Weighing up the Evidence

HOW AND WHY:

The
Third
Reich

Nigel Richardson

Dryad Press Ltd London

Contents

	Introduction – 1945	3
Part One:	**The Story of the Third Reich, 1933-39**	6
Part Two:	Filling in the Background:	
	Defeated Germany, 1918	18
	The Weimar Republic, 1918-29	23
	Hitler's Early Life and Career, 1918-29	28
	The Republic collapses, 1929-33	33
Part Three:	**Hitler sets up the One-Party State, 1933-34**	39
Part Four:	**"Co-ordination": Events in Germany, 1933-39**	42
Part Five:	**Foreign Policy and Rearmament**	45
Part Six:	**German Resistance to Hitler**	49
Part Seven:	**Hitler and the Jews**	52
	Epilogue – 1939-45	55
	Sources	58
	Biographies	59
	Glossary	61
	Date List	63
	Index	64

ACKNOWLEDGMENTS
The author and publishers thank the following for their kind permission to reproduce copyright illustrations: BBC Hulton Picture Library, page 21; Bundesarchiv, pages 12, 14, 23, 26, 44; Imperial War Museum, page 36; National Archives, page 4 (bottom); Panstwowe Muzeum Oswiecim, Poland, page 10; The Photo Source, pages 11, 15, 29, 31, 38 (left); *Punch*, pages 38 (right), 47; The Robert Hunt Library, pages 4 (top), 8, 34, 42, 55; The Wiener Library, page 54. The map on page 20 is by R.F. Brien.
 The pictures on the front cover are reproduced courtesy of the Mary Evans Picture Library (top left); The Wiener Library Photo Archives (top right) and The Photo Source (bottom).
 Extracts from Jeremy Noakes and Geoffrey Pridham, *Documents on Nazism 1919-1945* (Jonathan Cape Ltd) are reprinted by permission of A.D. Peters and Co Ltd.

© Nigel Richardson 1987   First published 1987
Typeset by Tek-Art Ltd, Kent
and printed in Great Britain by R.J. Acford Ltd, Chichester, Sussex
for the Publishers, Dryad Press Limited,
8 Cavendish Square, London W1M 0AJ

Introduction – 1945

In the mines, where the basement cellars had defied all the bombs, people were quick off the mark to take possession of any four walls still standing, even if they were half underground. The cellars would soon be cleared of any debris, a ceiling fixed up and windows put in; enough building material was lying around anyway, free for the taking. Having managed to make some sort of living quarters habitable, one would find they were surprisingly comfortable, considering the unusual circumstances; even little rags of curtains adorned the windows. It always struck me that these people were living like "little moles in their holes" but they were content for the time being. At least they had a makeshift roof over their heads. That was more than lots of other people had .... At that time, one could not, even with the wildest imagination, anticipate that any sort of civilisation would ever arise out of the ashes again.

(*Source:* Paula Kühl, describing Hamburg after the Allied bombing raid of 1943, quoted in *The Battle of Hamburg*, Martin Middlebrook, Allen Lane, 1980)

When the Second World War ended in Europe, one minute after midnight on 8 May 1945, Germany lay in almost total ruin. Seven million Germans were dead – a third of them civilians. Many of those who were still alive had lost everything. The German army had almost disintegrated; one British officer who helped to receive surrendering soldiers near Hamburg described "its pride broken, its endurance at an end. Old and elderly men who could hardly walk plodded along with the aid of sticks, or sat down by the roadside resting their tired feet and nibbling at a crust of bread; boys of fourteen or fifteen scowled sullenly or looked bewildered; others slouched along in silence, their arms long since thrown away . . ." (quoted in *The Battle of Hamburg*).

Two-thirds of cities like Berlin and Cologne had been flattened. Farms, railways, roads, water and drainage systems had been destroyed; typhus and other deadly diseases threatened the whole population. Wild animals roamed the countryside, while ex-prisoners-of-war from other countries, who had been brought to Germany as slaves, terrorized the streets. Food was very scarce, and those who sold it charged sky-high prices. "I never saw such destruction," said American President Harry Truman when he visited Berlin in 1945.

Adolf Hitler, the dictator who had ruled Germany from 1933 until only a few days earlier had promised that it would all be so different. He had come to power boasting that he would make Germany great again after her defeat in 1918, that he would put an end to the unemployment from which so many Germans had suffered in the 1920s. His Third Reich, or Empire, would achieve even greater successes than the two great German empires of earlier times.

When Hitler was just a small-time politician with very few supporters in the late 1920s, most people believed that he would never be a serious

Hitler in Munich in the early 1930s.

threat to anyone because he would never gain power. His earlier attempt to seize it (in 1923) had been a hopeless failure. Even as late as December 1929 the British magazine *The Listener* wrote that "the German Republic is pretty nearly as stable and solid as any other regime on the Continent".

Yet barely three years later Hitler was Germany's Chancellor. Within a year of that, all opposition to him had been ruthlessly crushed and his huge secret police force, Heinrich Himmler's SS, had complete control over the civilian population. The Nazis controlled every newspaper, every radio broadcast, every newsreel film, and every aspect of German life. For six years after 1933 Hitler also rearmed Germany, in direct defiance of the

June 1945: Nuremburg devastated.

Versailles Treaty, and seized territory abroad. His old enemies, Britain and France, did little to resist him until finally in September 1939, when German troops marched into Poland, they realized that he had got to be halted before it became too late to stop him at all.

In the years since 1945 historians have studied the evidence, asking themselves how it was ever allowed to happen. How could a madman like Hitler win the enthusiastic support even of many educated Germans — industrialists and intellectuals? How could men like British Prime Minister Neville Chamberlain have believed that he was a reasonable man whose demands could be satisfied? How could some Germans, and some of those abroad who watched what was going on in Germany, have convinced themselves that the Jews were not being persecuted and later not being killed in millions? How could they remember the children in the Hitler Youth movement, but ignore the plight of those in the concentration camps? Historical investigations will never produce an answer that historians can all agree about, but their work is very important. Understanding how and why Hitler came to power and then used it with such appalling cruelty may help us all to ensure that such a thing never happens again.

This book begins with an examination of the main features of Hitler's government between his appointment as Chancellor in 1933 and the start of Germany's war against Britain six years later. You need to work out why it proved so difficult to resist him and why his opponents both at home and abroad consistently under-estimated his true aims and the ruthless methods he was prepared to use in achieving them. The "Filling in the Background" section then aims to explain why Hitler was allowed to come to power in the first place. The final sections of the book examine various aspects of the Nazi regime in more detail. At the back of the book you will find a glossary which explains difficult terms and a section of brief biographies of leading figures of the period.

Historians dispute the extent to which Hitler worked out his ideas and his timetable for carrying them out in the years before he became Chancellor, and how like or unlike previous dictators he was — particularly in his obsession with Race and in his exploitation of the mass media (radio, newspapers and cinema). There is also plenty of argument about how much blame the Allied leaders must bear for causing the war by not standing up to Hitler earlier in the 1930s. This book aims to help you make up your own mind by weighing up the evidence about these and many other issues.

The Story of the Third Reich, 1933–39

1933 HITLER BECOMES GERMAN CHANCELLOR

Appeal to the German People by Hitler, 31 January:

Over fourteen years have passed since that unhappy day when the German people, blinded by promises made by those at home and abroad, forgot the highest values of our past, of the Reich, of its honour and freedom and thereby lost everything . . .

The task before us is the most difficult which has faced German statesmen in living memory.

The National Government will therefore regard it as its first and supreme task to restore to the German people unity of mind and will. It will take under its firm protection Christianity as the basis of our morality, and the family as the nucleus of our nation and our state. Germany must not and will not sink into Communist anarchy . . .

The Marxist parties and their followers had fourteen years to prove their abilities. The result is a heap of ruins. Now, German people, give us four years and then judge us.

(*Source:* Quoted in *Documents on Nazism 1919-45*, Jeremy Noakes and Geoffrey Pridham, Jonathan Cape, 1974)

In that speech, Hitler showed his determination to make a clean break with two major features of Germany's recent past, the Treaty of Versailles of 1919 and the Republican governments of 1919-33. Within a few weeks, he introduced an Enabling Bill which would give the cabinet the power to pass laws without Parliament's (the Reichstag's) approval. Hitler's political opponents were closely watched by his supporters in the SA and SS, the stormtroopers and the secret police, as the debate on this bill took place.

1933: HITLER'S ENABLING ACT GIVES HIM SWEEPING POWERS

A Socialist member of the Reichstag describes the Parliamentary debate:

. . . The wide square in front of the Kroll Opera House was crowded with dark masses of people. We were received with wild choruses: 'We want the Enabling Act!' Youths with swastikas on their chests eyed us insolently, blocked our way, in fact made us run the gauntlet, calling us names like 'Centre pig', 'Marxist sow' . . . . The assembly hall was decorated with swastikas and similar ornaments. When we Social Democrats had taken our seats on the extreme left, SA and SS men lined up at the exits and along the walls behind us in a semicircle. Their expressions boded no good.

Hitler read out his government declaration in a surprisingly calm voice. Only in a few places did he raise it to a fanatical frenzy: at the end of his speech, he uttered dark threats of what would happen if the Reichstag did not vote the Enabling Act he was demanding . . .

Otto Wels read out our reply. With his voice half choking, he gave our good wishes to the persecuted and oppressed in the country who, though innocent, were already filling the prisons and concentration camps simply on account of their political creed.

This speech made a terrifying impression on all of us. Only a few hours before, we had heard that members of the SA had taken away the 45-year-old welfare worker, Maria Janovska of Köpenick, to a National Socialist barracks, stripped her completely, bound her on a table and flogged her body with leather whips. The female members of our group were in tears, some sobbed uncontrollably . . .

But Hitler jumped up furiously and launched into a passionate reply.

We tried to dam the flood of Hitler's unjust accusations with interruptions of 'No!', 'An error!', 'False!' But that did us no good. The SA and SS people, who surrounded us in a semicircle along the walls of the hall, hissed loudly and murmured: 'Shut up!', 'Traitors!', 'You'll be strung up today'.

(*Source:* William Hoegner, 1963, quoted in *Documents on Nazism 1919-45*, Noakes and Pridham)

1933: GERMANY OFFICIALLY BECOMES A ONE-PARTY STATE

Soon after the Enabling Act became law, Hitler used it to abolish all other political parties.

Law against the Establishment of Parties, 14 July 1933:

Article I   The National Socialist German Workers' Party constitutes the only political party in Germany.

Article II   Whoever undertakes to maintain the organisation of another political party or to form a new political party shall be punished with penal servitude of up to three years or with imprisonment of between six months and three years, unless the act is subject to a heavier penalty under other regulations.

(*Source:* Quoted in *Documents on Nazism 1919-45*, Noakes and Pridham)

1933: THE TERROR CONTINUES

Political opponents were already being rounded up by local Nazi officials. Three camps to house them were set up in 1933, including one at Dachau, near Munich. Others soon followed.

A local police chief describes life in an early concentration camp:

Only when the SS group leader in Düsseldorf had given the commandant permission by telephone was I allowed to enter the camp. But what can an 'inspection' of such an institution reveal? The prisoners' replies to the questions by the inspector are determined by the fear of displeasing their tormentors in whose power the prisoners remain. The food is always adequate and the shining cleanliness of floors and barracks and the scrupulous tidiness of the beds do not tell that they are a means of tormenting the inmates.

(*Source:* Rudolf Diels, 1950, quoted in *Documents on Nazism 1919-45*, Noakes and Pridham)

1934: HITLER'S STORMTROOPERS PURGED IN NIGHT MASSACRE

Hitler's stormtroopers, the SA, included many of his earliest supporters. But by 1934 they were becoming difficult to control. Street violence grew alarmingly. Fearing that the army generals might rise against him, Hitler decided that the SA must be wiped out. He later claimed that the SA leader, Ernst Röhm had been plotting against him.

An American journalist describes the slaughter:

At the moment of 2 am on June 30th when Hitler was taking off from Berlin, Captain Röhm and his SA lieutenants were peacefully slumbering in their beds at the Hanslbauer Hotel at Wiessee.

Edmund Heines, the SA Obergruppenführer of Silesia, a convicted murderer, was in bed with a young man. So far did the SA chiefs seem from staging a revolt (as Hitler later claimed) that Röhm had left his staff guards in Munich. There appeared to be plenty of carousing among the SA leaders but no plotting . . .

Shortly after dawn Hitler and his party sped out of Munich towards Wiessee in a long column of cars. They found Röhm and his friends still fast asleep in the Hanslbauer Hotel. The awakening was rude. Heines and his young male companion were dragged out of bed, taken outside the hotel and summarily shot on the orders of Hitler.

Hitler, in a final act of what he apparently thought was grace, gave orders that a pistol be left on the table of his old comrade. Röhm refused to make use of it. 'If I am to be killed, let Adolf do it himself', he is reported to have said. Thereupon two SA officers, according to the testimony of an eyewitness, entered the cell and fired their revolvers at Röhm point-blank. 'Röhm wanted to say something,' said this witness, 'but the SS officer motioned him to shut up. Then Röhm stood at attention – he was stripped to the waist – with his face full of contempt.' And so he died, violently as he had lived, contemptuous of the friend he had helped propel to the heights no other German had ever reached.

(*Source: The Rise and Fall of the Third Reich*, William L. Shirer, Pan Books, 1964)

Hitler reviewing the Stormtroopers, 1932. Röhm is on the left.

1934: PRESIDENT HINDENBURG DIES

A month later, the army generals, pleased at the removal of the SA, agreed to support the merging of the offices of President and Chancellor on the death of President Hindenburg. Hitler would henceforth be Führer (leader) of Germany.

Law that the armed forces must swear loyalty to Hitler and his successor:

Article I   The public officials and the soldiers of the armed forces must take an oath of loyalty on entering service.

Article II   The oath of loyalty of the soldiers of the armed forces will be:
   'I swear by God this sacred oath: I will render unconditional obedience to Adolf Hitler, the Führer of the German nation and people, Supreme Commander of the Armed Forces, and will be ready as a brave soldier to risk my life at any time for this oath.'

(*Source:* Quoted in *Documents on Nazism 1919-45*, Noakes and Pridham)

1935: HITLER BEGINS TO THINK POSITIVELY ABOUT FOREIGN EXPANSION

Hitler's long-term aim was completely to dismantle the 1919 Treaty of Versailles. But during his early years in power he was anxious to appear reasonable to Germany's old opponents.

Hitler meets British government leaders:

The Chancellor showed his British visitors a diagram indicating the comparative sizes of the European metropolitan countries . . . . He demonstrated that Germany, with a population density of 137 inhabitants to the square kilometre, had by herself insufficient economic living space. In the interests of true peace a solution must be sought which would be permanently acceptable. No-one in Germany, and least of all the National Socialists, felt any hatred or enmity towards Britain.

(*Source: Documents on German Foreign Policy 1919-1939*, HMSO, quoted in *Documents on Nazism 1919-45*, Noakes and Pridham)

1935: PERSECUTION OF GERMANY'S JEWS IS STEPPED UP

Hitler had always been fanatically against the Jews. Persecution of them began as soon as he came to power; two years later it was stepped up.

The Nuremburg Laws:

On 27 July 1935 Frick sent a memorandum to all states informing them that marriages between Aryans and non-Aryans would shortly be regulated by law. He instructed all registry offices to postpone not only such marriages but even their announcement . . . . Before long the Law for the Protection of German Blood and German Honour was completed. The provisions were simplicity itself: marriage between Jews and 'nationals of German kindred blood' was forbidden. Jews were forbidden to employ female domestic help under forty-five years who were of 'German or kindred blood'. Finally, Jews were forbidden to fly the

Early persecution of the Jews. Stormtroopers picket a Jewish shop: "Germans, beware! Do not buy from Jews!"

German national colours . . . . The Reich Citizenship Law distinguished between a subject and a citizen of the Reich.

(*Source: The War against the Jews 1933-45*, Lucy L. Dawidowicz, Pelican Books, 1977)

1936: GERMAN TROOPS MARCH INTO THE RHINELAND

One clause of the Versailles Treaty banned German troops from all the land which Germany controlled west of the River Rhine. In March 1936 Hitler felt strong enough to openly defy the clause.

The Government announcement:

In accordance with the fundamental right of a nation to secure its frontiers and ensure its possibilities of defence, the German government have today restored the full and unrestricted sovereignty of Germany in the demilitarised zone of the Rhineland . . .

The German government declares itself ready to conclude new agreements for the creation of a system of peaceful security for Europe.

(*Source:* Quoted in *Documents on Nazism 1919-45*, Noakes and Pridham)

1936: OLYMPIC GAMES HELD IN BERLIN

The Berlin Olympics of 1936 were one of the great showpieces of Nazi Germany, ruined for Hitler only by the success of athletes whom he regarded as racially inferior to Germans like the great American athlete, Jesse Owens, who won four gold medals.

Hitler fools his visitors:

Visitors who went to the festival came away enormously impressed, not only by the Olympic preparations, which were on a scale never seen before, but also by the fact that life seemed to go on as pleasantly as in any other European country. Many of them concluded that the tales they had heard about persecution of Jews, Catholics and political dissidents must have been grossly exaggerated, for as they moved around Berlin or drove freely through the country, they saw no signs of harassment; besides, the ordinary people they met were hospitable and kind. They came home convinced that the Nazi regime was far less black than it had been painted .... It was a triumph of bluff and propaganda ... by the Führer himself, executed largely by the genius of his Minister for Propaganda, Joseph Goebbels.... During the Games there was no single report of a foreign visitor being insulted on racial grounds. Neither Jewish athletes nor blacks were harassed or made to feel in the least degree unwelcome: on the contrary, all newcomers were received with overwhelming hospitality.

(*Source: Hitler's Games*, Dutt Hart-Davis, Century Hutchinson, 1986)

1936: THE FOUR-YEAR ECONOMIC PLAN

By 1936 the possibility of war to get the territory he wanted was increasingly in Hitler's mind. He decided that more urgent government action was needed in economic affairs, to prepare for this.

Recollections of Albert Speer, later Minister of Armaments:

The lack of understanding of the Reich Ministry for Economics and the opposition of German business to all large-scale plans induced Hitler .... to decide to carry out a Four-Year Plan and to put Göring in charge of it. On the occasion of Göring's appointment he gave him this memorandum:

"Politics are the conduct and the course of the historical struggle of nations for life. The aim of these struggles is survival .... Germany will as always have to be regarded as the force of the Western World against the attacks of Bolshevism.

"Parallel with the military and political rearmament for our nation ... must go its economic rearmament and mobilisation, and this must be effected in the same tempo, with the same determination, and if need be with the same ruthlessness as well."

(*Source: Documents on German Foreign Policy*, HMSO, quoted in *Documents on Nazism 1919-45*, Noakes and Pridham)

The torch lights the Olympic Flame at the Berlin Games, 1936.

1937: THE PEOPLE'S COURT

As the 1930s progressed, Hitler's government increasingly took over the powers of the traditional courts and of their judges. The so-called People's Court was the most notorious example.

American journalist William L. Shirer recalls life in Berlin:

On June 4 1937, I noted in my diary:

"Helmut Hirsch, a Jewish youth of twenty who was technically an American citizen though he had never been to America, was axed at dawn this morning. Ambassador Dodd fought for a month to save his life, but to no avail."

Hirsch was convicted and sentenced to death by the dreaded People's Court, an inquisitional tribune set up by the Nazis a couple of years before to try offenders against the state, of planning to murder Julius Streicher, editor of the scurrilous anti-Semitic weekly *Der Stürmer*, and an old pal of Hitler from the earliest party days.

I had attended a couple of trials before this so-called court – usually it acted in camera – and concluded that the accused seldom had a chance. Four of the five "judges" were party members (the fifth was a regular judge), the proceedings were a travesty of justice, with the members of the bench yelling accusations against their hapless victim and the poor state-appointed defense lawyers too cowed to argue their client's case. The defendants, no matter what the evidence, or lack of it, were invariably found guilty and almost as invariably sentenced to death.

(*Source: The Nightmare Years 1930-40*, William L. Shirer, Bantam Books, 1984)

1937: NAZI PROPAGANDA

Hitler was a master of techniques of persuading a mass audience. It was this skill, and his use of modern technology in staging rallies, that marked him out from earlier dictators.

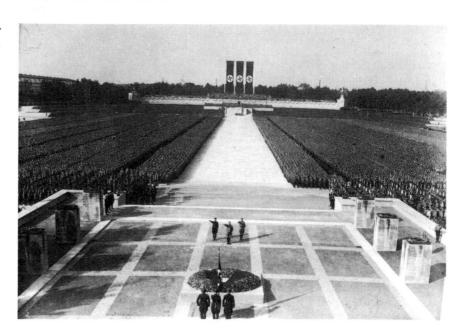

Hitler and Himmler at the Party Day Rally, Nuremburg, 1934.

The British Ambassador describes a Nazi rally:

Nobody who has not witnessed the various displays given at Nuremburg during the week's rally, or been subjected to the atmosphere thereat, can be said to be fully acquainted with the Nazi movement in Germany . . .

The displays themselves were most impressive. That of the Party leaders (or heads of the Party organisation in towns and villages throughout the country) took place in the evening at 8pm, in the stadium or Zeppelinfield. Dressed in their brown shirts, these 140,000 men were drawn up in six great columns, with passages between them, mostly in the stadium itself, but filling also the tiers of seats surrounding the stadium and facing the elevated platform reserved for the Chancellor, his Ministers and his guards, the massed bands, official guests, and other spectators. Hitler himself arrived at the far entrance of the stadium, some 400 yards from the platform, and, accompanied by several hundred of his followers, marched on foot up the central passage to his appointed place. His arrival was theatrically notified by the sudden turning into the air of the 300 or more searchlights with which the stadium was surrounded. The blue-tinged light from these met thousands of feet up in the sky at the top to make a kind of square roof, to which a chance cloud gave added realism. The effect, which was both solemn and beautiful, was like being inside a cathedral of ice. At the word of command the standard-bearers then advanced from out of sight at the far end, up the main lane, and over the further tiers and up the four side lanes. A certain proportion of these standards had electric lights on their shafts, and the spectacle of these five rivers of red and gold rippling forward under the dome of blue light, in complete silence, through the massed formations of brown shirts, was indescribably picturesque. As a display of aggregate strength it was ominous; as a triumph of mass organisation combined with beauty it was superb.

(Source: Sir Nevile Henderson, *Failure of a Mission, Berlin 1937-39*, Hodder and Stoughton, 1940)

1938: THE NAZIS PREPARED TO GO ON TO THE OFFENSIVE By early 1938 army leaders were increasingly fearful that Hitler was on a collision course with Britain and France. But Hitler, believing that these countries would do all they could to avoid another war, ruthlessly crushed all opposition to his policies.

How Hitler disgraced army leaders Blomberg and Fritsch, who were opposed to his aggressive foreign policy:

The trap was sprung by Himmler and Göring . . . . The trouble began with [General] Blomberg's eagerness to get married to a certain Fräulein Erna Grühn who, Blomberg admitted, was a lady "with a past". Aware of the shock this would give to the rigid views of the officer corps on the social suitability of the wife of a Field Marshal and a Minister of War, Blomberg consulted Göring as a brother-officer. Göring not only encouraged him but . . . when the marriage took place . . . Hitler and Göring were the principal witnesses . . .

At this stage . . . a police dossier was discovered which disclosed that the wife of the Field Marshal had a police record as a prostitute and had at one time been convicted of posing for indecent photographs . . . . Blomberg had dishonoured the Officer Corps . . .

For a long time Himmler had been looking for an opportunity to get rid of Fritsch . . . . Himmler and Göring settled the matter by again producing a police dossier, this time to show that General von Fritsch had been guilty of homosexual practices. They arranged for him to be confronted with Hans Schmidt, a young man who made his living by spying on and blackmailing well-to-do homosexuals.

Schmidt identified Fritsch as one of those from whom he had extorted money. In view of Schmidt's police record this was the flimsiest piece of evidence, and was later torn to shreds at the court of enquiry. The officer in question, it then emerged, was not Fritsch at all, but a retired cavalry commander of the name of Frisch. This fact was perfectly well known to the Gestapo, who later arrested Frisch in order to prevent the defence getting his evidence . . .

The trick had served its purpose . . . when the Cabinet met for the last time during the Third Reich on Monday 4 February . . . after announcing Blomberg's resignation, Hitler added than von Fritsch too, had asked to be relieved of his duties . . . on the grounds of ill-health.

(*Source: Hitler: A Study in Tyranny*, Alan Bullock, Pelican Books, 1962)

1938: THE "ANSCHLUSS": GERMANY ANNEXES AUSTRIA

The Nazis gained influence in the Austrian government and in March 1938, Austria became a province of Germany. In a referendum, 99.75 per cent of Austrians who voted were in favour of the union of the two countries.

Hitler speaks in the Austrian town of Linz, his home town:

When years ago I went forth from this town I bore within me precisely the same profession of faith which today fills my heart . . . . If Providence once called me forth from this town to be the leader of the Reich, it must,

Hitler with Generals Blomberg and Fritsch at the 1935 military exercises. Three years later, the two generals were disgraced.

in so doing, have charged me with a mission, and that mission could only be to restore my dear homeland to the German Reich. I have believed in this mission, I have lived and fought for it, and I believe I have now fulfilled it.

(*Source: The Speeches of Adolf Hitler 1922-39*, edited by Norman H. Baynes, OUP, 1942)

1938: CRYSTALNIGHT

By 1938 the plight of the Jews in Germany was becoming increasingly desperate.

Mass destruction of Jewish property:

An unexpected opportunity for dealing with the Jews opened up with the assassination on 7 November of Ernst vom Rath, a third secretary in the German embassy in Paris, by a seventeen-year-old Polish Jewish student, Hershl Grynszpan.

In many small towns meetings were called on 8 or 9 November at which the party leader and the local mayor agitated the assembled mob, which then went into action, setting fire to the local synagogues, destroying Jewish businesses and homes and manhandling Jews.

Fires were ignited all over Germany, and shattered plate glass littered the streets of German towns and cities. Over 7000 Jewish businesses were destroyed. Nearly 100 Jews were killed, and thousands more subjected to wanton violence and sadistic torments.

Within a week Funk issued a circular letter to appropriate authorities declaring that Jewish businesses should not be reopened unless the management by non-Jews was assured. Where compensation was paid to Jews [by insurance companies] the German government would arrange to confiscate those payments.

(*Source: The War against the Jews*, Lucy L. Dawidowicz, Pelican Books, 1977)

Hitler enters the Sudetenland (Czechoslovakia) in triumph, 3 October, 1938

1939: THE FÜHRER IN CONFIDENT MOOD

By 1939 Hitler had taken over Austria and much of Czechoslovakia without a shot being fired. He had been proved right about the weakness of the Allies, and felt confident about the future.

Hitler looks back on his work so far:

I once took over a state which was faced by complete ruin . . . . I have conquered chaos in Germany, re-established order and enormously increased production . . . . I have succeeded in finding useful work for the whole of the seven million unemployed . . . . Not only have I united the German people politically, but I have also re-armed them. I have also endeavoured to destroy, sheet by sheet, that treaty which in its 448 articles contains the vilest oppression which peoples have ever been expected to put up with. I have brought back to the Reich provinces stolen from us in 1919. I have led back to their native country millions of Germans who were torn away from us and were in misery . . . and without spilling blood and without bringing to my people, and consequently to others, the misery of war.

(*Source: The Speeches of Adolf Hitler 1922-39*, edited by Norman H. Baynes, OUP, 1942)

1939: HITLER SIGNS AN AGREEMENT WITH COMMUNIST RUSSIA

Hitler had always reserved special hatred for Communism. In mid-1939 he astounded his enemies by signing an agreement with Stalin's Russia.

The alliance with Russia:

On 22 August Ribbentrop flew to Moscow, with Hitler's authority to divide up Poland and Eastern Europe with Russia, and the agreement signed on the 23rd included a secret annex which contained the details of this division of spoils:

The Government of the German Reich
and
The Government of the Union of Soviet Socialist Republics,

directed by the wish to strengthen the cause of peace between Germany and the USSR . . . have reached the following agreement:
Article 1 The two contracting parties undertake to refrain from any act of violence, any aggressive action, or any attack against one another, whether individually or jointly with other powers . . .

. . . the two parties discussed in strictly confidential conversations . . . their respective spheres of influence in Eastern Europe. These conversations led to the following result:

Article 2 In the event of a territorial and political transformation of the territories belonging to the Polish State, the spheres of interest of both Germany and the USSR shall be bounded approximately by the line of the rivers Narev, Vistula and San . . .

(*Source: Documents on German Foreign Policy*, HMSO, quoted in *Documents on Nazism 1919-45*, Noakes and Pridham)

1939: THE ROAD TO WAR

The Treaty of Versailles had divided Germany into two separate areas of land by creating a "corridor" of land for Poland to the Baltic port of Danzig (see map on page 20). In September 1939 Hitler again defied the Allies and decided to redraw the map of Europe once more.

Hitler invades Poland:

On the roads the continuous traffic of war rolled along, lorries, armoured cars, tanks, motorcycles, all moving towards the front. And in the opposite direction, the unending stream of prisoners, exhausted by battle . . .

After landing very near Warsaw, we inspected two heavily damaged Polish armoured trains which had been put out of action by Stukas. Hitler climbed about among the wreckage, inspecting everything very closely . . . . He personally measured the thickness of the train's armour plate with a ruler, and inspected the armament, the calibre of the guns etc . . . .

Upon the capitulation of the city on 29 September, we travelled to Warsaw by road . . . . I was shocked at what had become of the most beautiful city I had known – ruined and burnt-out houses, starving and grieving people . . . . Everywhere there was the sweetish smell of burnt flesh. There was no running water anywhere . . . . Warsaw was a dead city.

(*Source: The Schellenberg Memoirs*, Walter Schellenberg, André Deutsch, 1956)

1939: BRITAIN DECLARES WAR

Britain and France had learned from Hitler's earlier aggressive acts, and had promised to protect Poland. On 3 September, Britain declared war on Germany.

The Prime Minister's broadcast to the German people, 4 September:

He gave his word that he would respect the Locarno Treaty; he broke it. He gave his word that he neither wished nor intended to annex Austria; he broke it. He declared that he would not incorporate the Czechs in the Reich; he did so. He gave his word after Munich that he had no further territorial demands in Europe; he broke it. He gave his word that he wanted no Polish provinces; he broke it. He has sworn to you for years that he was the natural enemy of Bolshevism; he is now its ally.

Can you wonder his word is, for us, not worth the paper it is written on?

(*Source: Documents concerning German-Polish relations and the outbreak of hostilities between Great Britain and Germany on September 3rd 1939*, HMSO, 1939)

Filling in the Background: Defeated Germany, 1918

To understand why Germans eventually turned to Hitler in large numbers, we have to begin with the First World War. Defeat for the Germans in 1918 came as a terrible disappointment – and a great shock. From 1860-90, under Chancellor Otto von Bismark, Germany had won a series of dazzling victories in Europe. From 1890-1914 Kaiser (Emperor) Wilhelm II encouraged his people to believe that their armies would always be victorious and that, as a major power, Germany deserved more territory. The outbreak of war in 1914 strengthened this optimistic belief. University professors and military leaders were keen to spread the idea, even though some politicians had doubts.

German dreams of land gains in 1914:

The Parliamentary bloc that controlled the Reichstag in the first two years of the war . . . were impassioned supporters of a programme of extensive claims in both Eastern and Western Europe . . . . Matthias Erzberger in September 1914 was so intoxicated by the dream of victory that he drafted a memorandum in which he called for the annexation of all of Belgium plus the Channel coast as far as Boulogne . . . . Hermann Schuhmacher sought support for the German acquisition of Calais by arguing 'Calais is really a very small port. The French will never miss it.'

(*Source: Germany 1866-1945*, Gordon Craig, OUP 1978)

When Germany faced defeat in the summer of 1918, the generals tried to shift the blame on to the Emperor and the politicians. The army set up a civilian government which they hoped would be more acceptable to the victorious powers than the previous one and would persuade them not to demand harsh terms when peace came. A month later, with the armed forces in revolt and with the threat of a Communist takeover a real possibility, Wilhelm II abdicated and fled abroad, and Germany stopped fighting.

THE GERMAN REPRESENTATIVES AT VERSAILLES

In April 1919 the Allies summoned German representatives to meet them at Versailles, near Paris. The diplomats who went were representatives of the new, civilian government; few of them had played any part in the war itself. They were horrified to discover that there were to be no negotiations; the victorious powers would dictate terms which could not be questioned.

Dr Walter Simons, a senior civil servant in the German foreign office, was one of the expert advisers who travelled with the diplomats by train to France. He described his experiences in a series of letters to his wife.

The German delegates travel to France, April/May 1919:

Then, however, came Northern France! It was an overwhelming experience, even if we know from pictures and descriptions what a battlefield looks like. The greater part of the day the train was intentionally slowed down when passing through this bomb-torn, desolate country which once bore such rich fruit; past the ruins of villages and towns in which one saw almost no one, nothing but clean-up detachments at work. We crossed emergency bridges the predecessors of which were lying in the river below us. We stopped at stations between collapsed buildings, burned sheds, and exploded munition trains, until we had seen all we could endure . . . . The guards generally tolerated the acclamations and the handwavings of the prisoners; although one of them, when a German standing near him called out, hit him on the head with the butt of his rifle. Some of the Germans were quartered in freight cars, others in dugouts, and still others in tents. The dugouts looked very damp and unhealthy as far as one could judge from the railway. Many French soldiers and civilians were also occupied with the work of restoration.

It struck me that the Germans seemed to suffer from cold as much as the colonial troops, whereas the French seem to be less affected by the weather. This may be a symptom of undernourishment.

(*Source: The German Delegation at the Paris Peace Conference*, Alma Luckau, Columbia University Press, 1941)

The Allies met the German representatives in the Hall of Mirrors at the Palace of Versailles, seventeen miles outside Paris, on 7 May 1919. It was a brief, cold meeting at which the Germans were given a copy of the Treaty and told to go back to their hotel to study it. Discovering its details came as a terrible shock. They were especially critical of American President Woodrow Wilson who, they believed, had promised that the Treaty would be a moderate one. The Treaty threatened an invasion by Allied troops if the Germans failed to fulfil its terms.

Dr Simons describes the meeting with the Allied leaders:

The German table had already been designated as 'banc des accusés' [defendants' bench] . . . . The British feigned boredom and indifference. Lloyd George laughed and Bonar Law yawned . . . . The Treaty is a monument of pathological fear and hatred . . .

(*Source: The German Delegation at the Paris Peace Conference*, Alma Luckau, Columbia University Press, 1941)

THE TERMS OF THE TREATY

Land in Europe:

Germany lost Alsace-Lorraine to France. The French were also to control the Saar region for fifteen years. Both these areas had rich reserves of coal. In the East, a huge slice of German land was given to Poland. This gave the Poles a port – Danzig – but cut off Germany's most easterly province, East

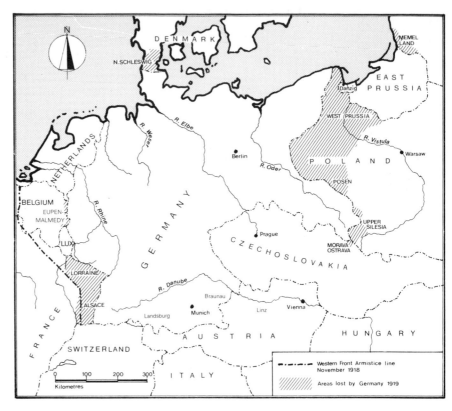

Prussia, from the rest of Germany. The map shows details of these and other, minor changes.

Colonies:

Germany lost all her overseas colonies and all the property in them.

Armed forces:

Germany's army was to be limited to 100,000 men. There were to be no German military aircraft, tanks, large warships or submarines. The Allies would seize large quantities of military equipment and munitions.

Other restrictions:

Union of Germany and Austria was forbidden. No German troops were to be allowed to enter the Rhineland – that area of Germany nearest to the French border.

Compensation:

Germany was to pay a sum later fixed at £6,600 million to Belgium and France. This was justified by the most controversial clause in the whole treaty:

Outside Berlin, 1919, a German tank being broken up after the Treaty of Versailles.

Article 231:

The Allied and Associated Governments affirm and Germany accepts the responsibility of Germany and her allies for causing all the loss and damage to which the Allied and Associated Governments and their nationals have been subjected as a consequence of the war imposed on them by the aggression of Germany and her Allies.

(*Source: Documents in the Political History of the European Continent 1915-1939*, G.A. Kertesz, Clarendon Press, 1968)

THINGS TO DO AND THINK ABOUT:

Look back at the quotation from Gordon Craig's book on page 18. Why do you think he emphasizes the extent of German territorial hopes in 1914?

How many arguments can you think of to support the German view that the Treaty was too harsh? What would the Allied reply have been to those arguments? As you read on, think carefully about whether the Allies were wise or not to draw up this sort of treaty.

REACTIONS TO THE TREATY WITHIN GERMANY . . .

The treaty did a great deal to undermine the new German government. The newspapers led a furious outcry against it.

A German newspaper editorial:

VENGEANCE! GERMAN NATION!

Today in the Hall of Mirrors of Versailles the disgraceful Treaty is being signed. Do not forget it! The German People will, with unceasing labour, press forward to reconquer the place among the nations to which it is entitled. Then will come vengeance for the shame of 1919.

(*Source: Deutsche Zeitung*, 28 June 1919)

Dr Simons also described the angry prophecy of one of the German delegates a few hours after the treaty had been presented by President Wilson of the USA, Lloyd George of Britain, and Clemenceau of France.

Giesberts vows revenge:

He staggered somewhat, dropped into a chair, and said:

"Gentlemen, I am drunk. This shameful treaty has broken me, for I had believed in Wilson until today. From that day I believed him to be an honest man, and now that scoundrel sends us such a treaty. Right now if I had those fellows here, who this afternoon were sitting opposite me – Wilson, Lloyd George, and Clemenceau – they would hit the ceiling so hard that they'd stick to it. But I am telling you this, gentlemen (and with that he jumped up and banged his fist on the table so hard that it spilled my glass of cognac) if those fellows think that the German laborers are going to work hard for that capitalist gang, they're wrong, and when they march into the mining district, the few hand grenades that'll be needed to flood every mine, will be on hand!"

(*Source: The German Delegation at the Paris Peace Conference*, Alma Luckau, Columbia University Press, 1941)

. . . AND WITHIN BRITAIN

The Times **warns about the continuing danger from Germany:**

If there is one country that the Germans are determined to get even with it is France . . .

(*Source: The Times*, 30 June 1919)

Over the next fifteen years, the Germans succeeded in having reparations reduced, but the Allies refused to end them altogether until 1932. By then, it was too late; the new German republic had become so unpopular that it was about to collapse.

Filling in the Background: The Weimar Republic, 1918-29

THE NEW GOVERNMENT
When Germany surrendered in 1918, a Republic was proclaimed, led by the moderate socialist, Friedrich Ebert. The new government faced crippling

A Berlin barracks, 9 November 1918. Members of a socialist workers' council want the troops to refuse to fight any longer in a capitalist war. They carry a placard saying "Brothers, don't shoot!"

problems from the very start – strikes, demonstrations and mutiny in some units of the armed forces. The Communists hoped quickly to overthrow it, and to establish an extreme left-wing government like the one which had recently come to power in Russia, under Lenin. Right-wingers, who believed strongly in patriotism and who hated anything to do with Communism or Russia, distrusted any socialist government – even a moderate one.

THE SPARTAKIST REVOLT
A month after the war ended, the Communists briefly seized power in the southern state of Bavaria. In January 1919 they staged their "Spartakist" revolt in the capital itself, Berlin. After three days of bitter street fighting the government crushed the revolt, with the help of the army and the Freikorps

– groups of right-wing ex-soldiers who formed unofficial units and enthusiastically massacred over 1500 Communists in several German cities.

Later in 1919 the government became alarmed at the growing lawlessness of the Freikorps and decided to dissolve them. Leading generals declared that the army was sympathetic to them and that the government could not rely on any support against them. The government had to leave Berlin altogether for a time – a takeover plot hatched by Dr Wolfgang Kapp failed because workers called a general strike against it. It was only then that the army decided to back the government, rather than let Germany sink into chaos. Thus, within its first six months of life, the new Republic was seen by everyone to be dangerously fragile.

THE WEIMAR CONSTITUTION

In February 1919 a National Assembly of politicians met in the old German town of Weimar and appointed Ebert as President. Over the next six months it drew up a new constitution for Germany.

Two views of the Weimar Constitution:

It is obvious that the first decisions at Weimar mean that Germany is now governed by the old Reichstag . . . and that all the Federal states start fresh with their old rights safeguarded. And the German government is in the hands of the old politicians. German liberal organs [newspapers etc] admit that it is a very bad start, and that the prospects of reform are poor . . .

(*Source: The Times*, 18 February 1919)

The constitution which emerged from the Assembly after six months of debate was, on paper, the most liberal and democratic document of its kind that the twentieth century had seen, mechanically well-nigh perfect, full of ingenious and admirable devices which seemed to guarantee the working of an almost flawless democracy.

(*Source: The Rise and Fall of the Third Reich*, William L. Shirer, Pan Books, 1964)

However perfect the new constitution appeared on paper, in practice it contained some features which caused grave problems later on. Article 48 gave the President strong emergency powers. Can you think how this might prove to be dangerous when the President became old or ill? How could it be exploited? Hitler would later take advantage of this point. The precise relationship between the central government and the individual state governments was never properly worked out. Hitler would later be able to play on disagreements between them. Above all, the proportional representation system of voting which they chose meant that no single party would ever have a majority over all its rivals combined, in the German parliament, the Reichstag. Government under the Weimar system became a series of coalitions between several parties, and firm decisive action was very hard to achieve.

Elections for the Reichstag 1919-33:

Party	May 1924	Dec 1924	May 1928	Sept 1930	July 1932	Nov 1932	March 1933
Social Democratic	100	131	152	143	133	121	120
Independent Socialist	–	–	–	–	–	–	–
Communist	62	45	54	77	89	100	81
Catholic Centre	65	69	61	68	75	70	73
Bavarian People's	16	19	17	19	22	20	19
Hanoverian	5	4	3	3	–	1	–
People's	44	51	45	30	7	11	2
Democrat	28	32	25	14	4	2	5
Economic	9	17	23	23	2	1	–
Independents	5	–	–	51	7	10	6
Nationalist	106	103	79	41	40	51	53
National Socialist	32	14	12	107	230	196	288
TOTAL	472	485	471	576	609	583	647

1. Candidates were elected on the proportional representation system which gave the smaller parties a chance to win seats.
2. The number of seats was determined by the total number of votes cast in each election.

(*Source: Hitler and the Rise of the Nazis*, D.M. Phillips, The Archive Series, Hill and Fell, Edward Arnold, 1968)

ECONOMIC PROBLEMS

The new government was blamed for the unpopular Versailles Treaty, and many people looked back longingly to the pre-war past. There was worse to come. In 1921, when the full size of the German reparations bill became public, the German *Mark* began to lose value against foreign currencies. It soon became completely worthless.

Number of Marks per American dollar:

	1914	4.2
January	1919	8.9
January	1920	64.8
November	1921	70
January	1922	192
January	1923	18,000
July		160,000
August		1,000,000
September		98,860,000
October		25,260,208,000
November 15		4,200,000,000,000

(*Source: Germany*, Robert Gibson and John Nichol, Blackwell, 1985)

The cost of one loaf of bread in Berlin:

	1918	0.63 *Marks*
	1922	163 *Marks*
January	1923	250 *Marks*
July	1923	3,465 *Marks*
September	1923	1,512,000 *Marks*
November	1923	201,000,000,000 *Marks*

(*Source: Weimar Germany*, Josh Brooman, Longman, 1986)

One German woman went to buy a few groceries from her local shop. She took a laundry basket full of banknotes to pay for them, and put the basket down while she opened the shop door. When she looked up, the notes were at her feet, but the basket had been stolen – it was more valuable than the notes!

The despair of an unemployed German.

A personal experience of German inflation, 1923:

A soon as I received my salary I rushed out to buy the daily necessities. My daily salary, as editor of the periodical *Soziale Praxis*, was just enough to buy one loaf of bread and a small piece of cheese or some oatmeal. On one occasion I had to refuse to give a lecture at a Berlin city college because I could not be assured that my fee would cover the subway fare to the classroom, and it was too far to walk. On another occasion, a private lesson I gave to the wife of a farmer was paid somewhat better – by one loaf of bread for the hour.

An acquaintance of mine, a clergyman, came to Berlin from a suburb with his monthly salary to buy a pair of shoes for his baby; he could buy only a cup of coffee. The Zeiss works in Jena, a non-profit enterprise, calculated weekly earnings to be worth four gold marks, less than a sixth of prewar levels.

(*Source:* Dr. Frieda Wunderlich. Quoted in *Wages in Germany 1871-1945*, G. Bry, Princeton University Press, 1960)

Meanwhile, faced by financial chaos, the Germans had fallen behind with their reparations payments. The French therefore sent troops into the Ruhr to seize coal instead; there was a general strike, rioting and even some executions before the French withdrew. Again, people blamed the government.

ORDER IS RESTORED

Eventually order was restored and a new German currency was introduced. Between 1924 and 1929 the Americans lent millions of dollars to Germany and this enabled industry to be modernized, houses and new towns to be built. Under Foreign Minister Gustav Streseman, relations with the Allies were improved. Germany entered the League of Nations in 1926, and signed the international Kellogg Pact in 1928, agreeing never to use war as a means to achieve her territorial aims.

But 1923 had been an especially bad year for the Weimar Republic. Hitler had tried to overthrow it in Munich (as we shall see in the next chapter). Although he had failed, it was a gloomy sign for the future. Thousands of Germans who had no jobs, and therefore no trades unions to demand wage increases for them, self-employed small businessmen and pensioners living on their savings had been ruined and were very bitter. If bad times ever returned, they might well desert the political parties which supported the Weimar Republic and turn to politicians who were calling for more drastic measures. In 1929 the bad times did return – and by then, Hitler was well on his way to becoming a national figure in Germany.

THINGS TO DO AND THINK ABOUT:

See what you can find out about proportional representation systems and how they work. How do they differ from the British system?

Turn back to the two views about the Weimar Constitution on page 24. Are they direct contradictions or not? Can you explain why the two sources might see things so differently?

Filling in the Background: Hitler's Early Life and Career, 1918-29

HITLER'S EARLY LIFE

Adolf Hitler was born in Braunau, a small Austrian town, on 20 April 1889. His father, a customs official, was a very difficult man, and was frequently at loggerheads with young Adolf. He also had a disappointing time at school.

Hitler describes his teachers:

In 1924, while in prison, Hitler wrote a long rambling book, *Mein Kampf* ("My Struggle").

Our teachers were absolute tyrants. They had no sympathy with youth; their one object was to turn us into educated apes like themselves. If any pupil showed the slightest trace of originality, they persecuted him relentlessly.

(*Source: Mein Kampf*, Adolf Hitler, Hutchinson, 1969)

LIFE IN VIENNA

Hitler's desire to become an artist caused him to go to Vienna at the age of eighteen. He found life hard there too, and failed repeatedly to win a place at the Academy of Fine Arts. For five years he lived in hostels and shabby rooms, doing a series of odd jobs like snow-clearing. He was in no doubt about who to blame for his loneliness and poverty – the Jews. There were many in Vienna, some of them very rich.

Anti-semitism, the hatred of Jews, had been widespread in Europe in the Middle Ages and had revived in the late nineteenth century. Drawing on Charles Darwin's discovery that the human race evolved gradually through a biological struggle for existence, in which the strong always overcame the weak, the "Social Darwinists" argued that the same thing happened in social and political affairs. The modern state therefore had a duty, not to protect the weak, but to copy Nature and reject them, thus making its own position more secure. For most Social Darwinists this meant expelling supposedly "inferior" races like the Jews, so that they could no longer threaten the future of the vastly "superior" German-speaking people in Austria and in Germany itself. But for Hitler, these ideas eventually became a justification for trying to wipe out the Jewish race altogether. All this lay a long way in the future in his Vienna days, but he quickly became obsessed by the belief that it was the Jews who had caused the decline of Austria from its earlier greatness.

Hitler encounters a Jew for the first time:

I suddenly encountered an apparition in a black caftan and black sidelocks. 'Is this a Jew?' was my first thought. I observed the man furtively and cautiously, but the longer I stared at this foreign face, the more my question assumed a new form: 'Is this a German?' . . .

On putting the probing knife into the abscess, I found, like a maggot in a rotting body, a little Jew, often blinded by the sudden light . . . Was there any shady undertaking, any form of foulness . . . in which at least one Jew did not participate?"

(*Source: Mein Kampf*, Adolf Hitler, Hutchinson, 1969)

Hitler, in a crowd of cheering Germans in Munich, celebrating the outbreak of war, 1914.

HITLER AND THE FIRST WORLD WAR

In 1913 Hitler went to live in Munich. When the Great War began he joined the German army with great enthusiasm. He wrote later: "I sank down upon my knees and thanked Heaven out of the fullness of my heart for the favour of having been permitted to live at such a time." Although he rose only to the rank of Corporal, he won the Iron Cross, first class – for what reason is not known. He was wounded in the leg and temporarily blinded by poison gas. It was while recovering from the gas in hospital that he heard the news of Germany's defeat in 1918. Hitler was devastated.

Hitler's reaction to peace, 1918:

So it had all been in vain . . . all the sacrifices, the hours in which . . . we did our duty . . . in vain the death of 2 millions. Had they died for this, so that a gang of criminals could lay hands on the Fatherland? I now knew that all was lost. Only fools, liars and criminals could hope for mercy from the enemy. In these nights, hatred grew within me, hatred for those responsible for the deed. Miserable and degenerate criminals. My own fate now became known to me . . . . I decided to go into politics . . .

(*Source: Mein Kampf*, Adolf Hitler, Hutchinson, 1969)

THE NAZI PARTY IS BORN

After his recovery, Hitler returned to Munich. He got a job in the Army Political Department's Press and News Bureau, with the task of preventing socialist and pacifist ideas from taking root among the soldiers. On 12

September 1919 he went to investigate a meeting of the tiny German Workers' Party in a backroom of one of the city's beerhalls. There were only twenty or so people there, and the party had almost no money, but Hitler immediately joined it. Within a short time he had taken the party over, renamed it the National Socialists (Nazis) and was regularly speaking to audiences of hundreds, condemning Jews, socialists and the Versailles Treaty. The crooked cross "Swastika" was adopted as the party symbol. He received support from Captain Ernst Röhm, an important figure among the Freikorps. He began to develop his theories about how to be an effective speaker.

Hitler describes how to communicate with a mass audience:

The receptive power of the masses is very slight; their understanding is very restricted. On the other hand, they quickly forget. Such being the case, all effective propaganda must be confined to a few bare necessities . . . a few stereotyped formulae . . .

In the big lie, there is always a certain chance of credibility . . . in the primitive simplicity of their minds, they more readily fall for the big lie than the small one . . .

(*Source: Mein Kampf,* Adolf Hitler, Hutchinson, 1969)

Hitler wins an important recruit:

Hermann Göring was to become a key figure in Germany under Hitler. He attended an early Nazi meeting with his wife.

Göring could have enjoyed a life of comparative ease in Sweden but he felt the urge to return to Germany and help "wipe out the disgrace of Versailles – the shame of defeat, the corridor right through the heart of Prussia" . . .
　　. . . It wasn't until the autumn of 1922 at a mass meeting that he found someone worth following. It was a meeting at the Königsplatz protesting Allied demands to hand over alleged war criminals. A series of speakers from various parties took the platform. Then the crowd began calling out, "Hitler!" By chance he was standing near Göring and Carin, who had been married early that year, and they overheard him remark that he wouldn't think of addressing "these tame bourgeois pirates". Something about the man in the belted trench coat impressed Göring so much that he went to a party meeting at the Café Neumann. "I just sat unobtrusively in the background. Hitler wanted to build up a party that would make Germany strong and smash the Treaty of Versailles. 'Well,' I said to myself, 'that's the party for me! Down with the Treaty of Versailles, God damn it! . . .'"
　　At party headquarters he filled out a membership application.

(*Source: Adolf Hitler,* John Toland, Doubleday, 1976)

THE MUNICH PUTSCH, 1923　During the early 1920s the leaders of the state government of Bavaria hated the socialists who ran the central government in Berlin. In 1923, spurred on by German anger against the collapse of the *Mark* and the French invasion of the Ruhr, Hitler decided to try to seize power. He and a group of followers burst into a political meeting and "captured" three Bavarian leaders; but they escaped soon afterwards, and he was forced into a desperate gamble, a march on the city centre. Here the police lined up across the road and opened fire — several of Hitler's followers were killed, and Hitler himself was captured.

Hitler was put on trial in 1924, but received an extremely light sentence from a sympathetic judge — only five years in prison. He turned his trial into a triumph by using it to make powerful speeches which received plenty of publicity, and while in prison he wrote *Mein Kampf*.

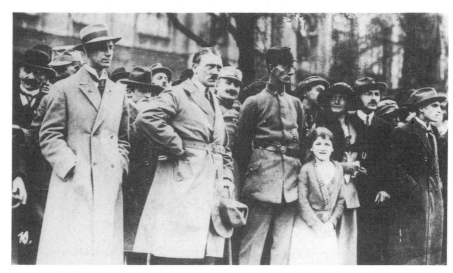

The early, difficult years. Hitler speaking in Munich, 1923.

THE YEARS OF STRUGGLE

While in prison, Hitler let his party almost disintegrate. He wanted to show his followers that they would never achieve anything without his leadership. After only nine months in a far from uncomfortable prison, Landsberg Castle, he was released. He set about completely reorganizing the party, dividing its organization across the country into 34 *Gaus* (districts), each controlled by a *Gauleiter*. He formed a personal bodyguard, the SS or *Schutzstaffeln* under Heinrich Himmler, which would later become his notorious secret police. He ruthlessly crushed all opposition to his policies, refusing even to consider another attempt to seize power by force. "Legal Revolution" was to be the tactic now — undermining the Weimar system from within by winning as many seats in parliament as possible. He firmly rejected the views of those who wanted to make the party more socialist, fearing that this would frighten off individualists who might give him money. And he would keep his promises as vague as possible, hoping thus to attract a wide degree of support. Otto Strasser, a Nazi who later broke with Hitler and went abroad, recalled an early argument about this.

Otto Strasser argues with Hitler:

I remember one of my first conversations with him. It was really our first quarrel.

"Power" screamed Adolf. "We must have power."

"Before we gain it, I replied firmly, "let us decide what we propose to do with it . . . ."

Hitler who even then could hardly bear contradiction, thumped on the table and barked: "Power first! Afterwards we can act as circumstances dictate."

(*Source: Hitler and I*, Otto Strasser, Cape, 1940)

THINGS TO DO AND THINK ABOUT:

Try to get hold of a copy of Hitler's book Mein Kampf *or extracts from it. (Many other books about this period of history include them; some are listed on page 58.) Study his description of his life up to 1924. How reliable an account do you think it is? How much does it explain his beliefs and his future actions?*

Filling in the Background: The Republic collapses, 1929-33

THE WALL STREET CRASH, 1929

Between 1924 and 1929 the German economy improved dramatically. This was largely due to loans from America. But in the autumn of 1929 the New York Stock Market collapsed – the notorious Wall Street Crash. American loans quickly stopped; German unemployment began to climb steeply again. In the same year the Allies agreed to scale down the reparations which Germany would have to pay, but refused to end them altogether. The new arrangements were known as the Young Plan.

Hitler quickly saw that he could win a lot of support by leading the opposition within Germany to the Young Plan. He joined forces with Alfred Hugenberg, the owner of a group of right-wing newspapers, who provided much of the money for the campaign. The Plan was approved, but six million voters opposed it in the referendum held in December 1929. Hitler had become a national figure; voters were slowly deserting the moderate parties.

HITLER GAINS SUPPORT

In July 1930 Hitler, Hugenberg, the Socialists and the Communists joined forces to defeat the budget proposed by Chancellor Brüning of the Roman Catholic Centre Party. In the election in the autumn, the Nazis sensationally increased their share of seats in the Reichstag from 12 to 107. The depression continued through 1931; several large banks failed and unemployment rose to six million. Hitler's speeches against the government, the Communists and the Versailles Treaty continued to win him support – especially from younger voters. His speech to the Düsseldorf Industry Club businessmen in January 1932 was especially successful. In it, he praised the determination of his followers.

Hitler addresses the industrialists:

... It means sacrifice when today many hundreds of thousands of SA and SS men of the National Socialist movement have every day to mount on their lorries, protect meetings, undertake marches, sacrifice themselves night after night and then come back in the grey dawn to workshop and factory, or as unemployed to take the pittance of the dole . . . . And if the whole German nation today had the same faith in its vocation as these hundreds of thousands, if the whole nation possessed this idealism, Germany would stand in the eyes of the world other than she stands now! (Loud applause).

(*Source: The Speeches of Adolf Hitler 1922-39*, Norman H. Baynes, OUP, 1942)

Hitler won equally enthusiastic support from ordinary Germans. Frau Louise Solnitz, a Hamburg schoolteacher married to a former army officer, described a party meeting in April 1932.

Hitler meets with SA members in Munich.

Hitler addresses the crowds in Hamburg:

There was immaculate order and discipline, although the police left the whole square to the stewards and stood on the sidelines. Nobody spoke of 'Hitler', always just 'the Führer', 'the Führer says', 'the Führer wants', and what he said and wanted seemed right and good. The hours passed, the sun shone, expectations rose. In the background, at the edge of the track there were columns of carriers like ammunition carriers. What they carried were crates of beer. Aeroplanes above us. Testing of the loudspeakers, buzzing of the cine-cameras. It was nearly 3pm. 'The Führer is coming!' A ripple went through the crowds. Around the speaker's platform one could see hands raised in the Hitler salute. A speaker opened the meeting, abused the 'system', nobody listened to him. A second speaker welcomed Hitler and made way for the man who had drawn 120,000 people of all classes and ages. There stood Hitler in a simple black coat and looked over the crowd, waiting – a forest of swastika pennants swished up, the jubilation of this moment was given vent in a roaring salute. Main theme: 'Out of parties shall grow a nation, the German nation. Thirteen years ago I was a simple unknown soldier. I went my way. I never turned back. Nor shall I turn back now.' Otherwise he made no personal attacks, nor any promises, vague or definite. His voice was hoarse after all his speaking during the previous days. When the speech was over, there was roaring enthusiasm and applause. Hitler saluted, gave his thanks, was helped into his coat. Then he went. – How many look up to him with touching faith! as their helper, their saviour, their deliverer from unbearable distress – to him who rescues the Prussian prince, the scholar, the clergyman, the farmer, the worker, the unemployed, who rescues them from the parties back into the nation.

(*Source:* Quoted in *Documents on Nazism 1919-45*, Noakes and Pridham)

NAZI STREET VIOLENCE

In reality, much of the energy of Hitler's followers was being used to terrorize Jews and Communists and to "persuade" people to support him. A particularly vicious example came to light in 1932:

The Potempa murder trial:

Five Nazis were sentenced to death today at Beuthen by a special summary court . . . for the killing of a communist named Pietzuch in his bedroom at Potempa near Beuthen. The gruesome story of the crime has already been transmitted; Pietzuch was beaten, shot and kicked to death by men who entered the room in which he, his brother, and his aged mother were asleep. The accused were not cast down, but exchanged friendly glances and Nazi greetings with the Nazi generalissimos present in court.

(*Source: The Times*, 23 August 1932)

Thanks to Hitler's moves behind the scenes, the sentences were reduced to life imprisonment.

A thirty-four-year-old SA member described his experiences in these years.

A stormtrooper talks of Nazi street violence:

In my work for the NSDAP [Nazis] I have faced a court more than thirty times and have been convicted eight times for assault and battery, resistance to a police officer and other such misdemeanours that are natural for a Nazi. To this day I am still paying instalments on my fines, and in addition have other trials coming up. Furthermore, I have been more or less severely wounded at least twenty times, I have knife scars on the back of my head, in my left shoulder, on my lower lip, on my right cheek, on the left side of my upper lip and on my right arm. Furthermore, I have never yet claimed or received a penny of Party money, but have sacrificed my time to our movement at the expense of the good business I inherited from my father. Today I am facing financial ruin.

(*Source:* Willi Veller's letter, dated 16 August 1930, quoted in *Hitler*, Joachim C. Fest, Pelican Books, 1977)

Violence could also take more subtle and less public forms. The Ministry for Churches and Schools in the state of Oldenburg received this complaint in November 1930 from a left-wing group, the Reichsbanner Black-Red-Gold.

Intimidation of schoolchildren:

Leaflets have recently been distributed in the playgrounds of the schools of the city of Oldenburg and its vicinity, inviting people to join a National Socialist Pupils' Association. We enclose one of these leaflets.

A number of pupils have already followed the appeal to join this pupils' association. These consider themselves pledged, in the spirit of the leaflet, to bully those who disagree with them. In the playground these pupils join together and sing National Socialist combat songs. Children of Republicans are called names, their satchels are smeared with swastikas, and they are given leaflets with swastikas or 'Heil Hitler' or 'Germany awake' written on them. In the school in Metjendorf the son of a Republican was beaten up during the break by members of the pupils' association so badly that he had to stay at home for over a week. Grown-ups who are known to be members of a Republican party are called names by the pupils when they pass by the school. In one case this even happened out of the window of a classroom.

Since the children of Republicans are unfortunately in a minority in secondary schools they cannot defend themselves against these combined attacks. With an effort they preserve their self-control, but as soon as the child gets home, this too collapses. He then seeks refuge in tears and complaints. The parents find that lessons following breaks in which their child has been molested by his classmates are useless because he is too preoccupied with the events of the break. Sometimes teachers, not knowing the reason for the child's inattention, punish him as well. The same state of mind influences his homework, which therefore cannot be of a standard which a child in a good, cheerful mood would normally achieve. Again this has its effects at school.

It might be answered that parents and children have the right to make a complaint. This is true and yet at the same time not true. It must unfortunately be said that apart from a group of teachers who would treat such a complaint objectively, there are a number from whom this cannot be counted on and to whom one does not turn because they too are National Socialists or are active in other right-wing associations. The relationship of trust necessary between teachers and parents and their children has completely gone.

(*Source:* Quoted in *Documents on Nazism 1919-45*, Noakes and Pridham)

Hitler's slogan "Only Hitler" for the 1932 presidential election led to this famous poster. He narrowly lost to Hindenburg.

THE NAZI BREAKTHROUGH

Thus Hitler was trying to destroy the Weimar Republic by violence, while presenting the image of a respectable politician using legal methods. All through 1931 and 1932 the Nazis held rallies and election meetings. Hitler used posters and films, travelling by plane to a schedule which no politician had ever attempted before. In April 1932 he stood as a candidate in the presidential election. The President since 1925 was Field Marshal Hindenburg, a hero of the First World War, and he wanted a second term of office. Hindenburg won, but Hitler polled over 13 million votes and the contest had to go to a second round with the Communist candidate dropping out after winning a mere 4 million supporters. Clearly, any government which wanted to survive long would have to depend on Hitler's approval.

In the summer of 1932 Chancellor Brüning was finally forced to resign. Franz von Papen, a friend of Hindenburg's, was appointed and told to form a "non-party" government. But Papen needed a majority in the Reichstag, in order to be able to get important legislation through, and called an election. The Nazis won 230 seats and thus became the largest single party.

These were nerve-wracking weeks for the Nazis. Goebbels' diary for the period around the election gives some idea of the tension.

Goebbels describes the growing political crisis, 1932:

30 May 1932 The bomb has exploded. Brüning has presented the resignation of the entire Cabinet to the President, at noon. The system has begun to crumble . . .

Von Papen is likely to be appointed Chancellor, but that is neither here nor there. The Poll! The Poll! It's the people we want . . .

2 June 1932 All through the morning and the afternoon we wait for news from Berlin. It arrives at four. The Opposition demands a written undertaking from the Führer that he will work smoothly with Papen even after the election. Such a statement cannot be made.

13 August 1932 The Führer is back in under half an hour. So it has ended in failure. He has gained nothing. Papen is to remain Chancellor and the Führer has to content himself with the position of Vice Chancellor.

(*Source: My Part in Germany's Fight*, Joseph Goebbels, London, 1938)

Hitler had indeed been to see the President to demand the chance to form a government and had been lectured by Hindenburg on his duty to support Papen. There seemed to be deadlock; several leading Nazis were urging Hitler to seize power by force, but he insisted on the need to work within the legal constitution. Papen called yet another election in November; this time the total of Nazi seats actually dropped (to 196), but they were still the largest party in the Reichstag.

Still Hitler refused to join the government unless given very wide powers. Hindenburg refused. But the ambitious General Schleicher convinced him that there was now a threat of a major political crisis and a general strike. If the strike took place, the Poles might seize the chance to invade. Schleicher became Chancellor – but only for 59 days. He had been sure that he could win over Gregor Strasser and the more radical Nazis, but he failed.

HITLER WINS POWER

In January 1933, Papen, still smarting from Schleicher's tactics, made Hitler a fateful offer. He would serve under Hitler as Vice-Chancellor. On 30 January Hitler was appointed Chancellor. "We have boxed him in," boasted Papen to his friends. It was one of the most fateful prophecies in history.

That evening the Nazis held a large victory rally through the streets of Berlin. Hitler had arrived.

Aged President Hindenburg speaking during 1933. This should have been a state occasion, but notice how Nazi Party uniforms and symbols dominate it.

FOR DEFENCE ONLY.

From Punch *magazine, 1932. The British begin to see the threat from Germany.*

THINGS TO DO AND THINK ABOUT:

How much do you think the Weimar Constitution itself was responsible for Hitler's rise to power?

Write down all the political skills you can detect in Hitler's conduct between 1918 and 1933.

Hitler sets up the One-Party State, 1933-34

When he became Chancellor in January 1933, there was no guarantee that Hitler would remain in office long. There were only three Nazi ministers in a cabinet of eleven, and the Nazis held less than half the seats in the Reichstag. The attitude of both President Hindenburg and the army towards him was uncertain. Yet eighteen months later he was totally powerful and all opposition had been ruthlessly crushed.

Hitler's first step was to force yet another election. Some other parties opposed this, but he promised them that the cabinet would not be altered, regardless of the result. He appealed to the people to support him (see page 6). During the election campaign, on 27 February, the Reichstag building mysteriously burned down.

HITLER SMASHES THE COMMUNISTS

The Reichstag building burns:

While the fire was still spreading, the police arrested a young Dutch communist, van der Lubbe, who was found in the building in circumstances which left little doubt that he was responsible . . . . The arrest of Communist leaders followed at once.

The convenience of the pretext led many to believe that the burning of the Reichstag was, in fact, planned and carried out by the Nazis themselves. A circumstantial version described how a band of Berlin SA men led by Karl Ernst penetrated into the deserted building by an underground tunnel and set the place ablaze. Van der Lubbe, who had been picked up by the SA after attempting to set fire to other buildings, was used as a dupe and allowed to climb into the Reichstag and start a fire on his own in another part.

Whichever version is accepted . . . the question, who started the fire? remains open, but there is no doubt about the answer to the question, who profited by it?

(*Source: Hitler: A Study in Tyranny*, Alan Bullock, Pelican Books, 1962)

Hitler now took emergency powers, according to the Weimar constitution.

Law restricting personal freedoms:

By the authority of Section 48 of the German Constitution the following is decreed as a defensive measure against Communist acts of violence endangering the State:

1. Sections 114, 115, 117, 118, 123, 124 and 153 of the Constitution are suspended until further notice. Thus restrictions on personal liberty, on the right of free expression of opinion, including freedom of the press, on the right of assembly and association, and violations of the privacy of

postal, telegraphic and telephonic communications, and warrants for house-searches, orders for confiscations . . . of property are permissible beyond the legal limits otherwise prescribed . . . .

(*Source:* Quoted in *Documents on Nazism 1919-45*, Noakes and Pridham)

Despite the fact that Communist leaders were blamed for the fire and immediately arrested, the Nazis gained only 43.9 per cent of the votes cast in the election. But as no Communists were allowed to take their seats in parliament, Hitler gained an absolute majority (more than half the total) over the rest. Less than a month later, the Enabling Bill was passed (see page 6). The Roman Catholic Centre Party dissolved itself in return for a written promise from Hitler that there would be freedom of worship, and no Nazi interference in Church affairs, that Church property would be protected and that Catholics could continue to run their own schools. The other political parties either followed its example or were forcibly closed down and their leaders fled abroad. The one-party state was officially declared in July (see page 7).

THE END OF LOCAL GOVERNMENT

Hitler also abolished local government, appointing Reich Governors to run each area. Purges began of the civil service, education, the law.

The Nazis seize power in Bavaria:

On the night of 9 March [1933] Adolf Wagner, the Gauleiter of Munich returned from strategy meetings in Berlin. While Hindenburg was still making reassuring promises and Hitler pretended ignorance, the Munich SA stood poised to force the resignation of the Bavarian government. Chief of Staff Röhm and Gauleiter Wagner appeared in Held's [the Bavarian chief minister's] office and presented him with an ultimatum to install General Ritter von Epp [as governor] . . . . Held tried to postpone a decision. But meanwhile armed SA and SS detachments were marching everywhere . . .

(*Source: The German Dictatorship*, K.D. Bracher, Penguin University Books, 1973)

Law for the Reconstruction of the Reich, 30 January 1934:

Article 1 Popular assemblies of the Federal States shall be abolished.

2(b) The Federal State governments are subordinated to the Reich government.

3 The Reich governors are placed under the administrative jurisdiction of the Reich minister of the interior.

(*Source:* Quoted in *Documents on Nazism 1919-45*, Noakes and Pridham)

HITLER BECOMES FÜHRER

Meanwhile Hitler had won at least the neutrality of army chiefs at a meeting on 2 February at which he promised them that he would rapidly rearm Germany (see part 5). They had longed for many years for the end of the armaments restrictions in the Treaty of Versailles and although they were wary of ex-corporal Hitler and his unruly band of followers, they were prepared – for the moment at least – to go along with him.

He met them again in April 1934, on the cruiser *Deutschland* where a crucial deal was agreed – he would succeed Hindenburg as President when the aged general died. In return, Hitler promised to suppress plans which Röhm was drawing up, which could effectively mean the army being taken over by the SA, and to recognize the army as the sole armed force in the State. Within weeks, the SA leadership had been massacred (see page 8).

Hitler justifies the massacre:

If anyone reproaches me and asks why I did not resort to the regular courts of justice for conviction of the offender, then all that I can say to him is this: in this hour I was responsible for the fate of the German people, and thereby I became the supreme Justiciar of the German people!

Everyone must know for all future time that if he raises his hand to strike the State, then certain death is his lot.

(*Source: The Speeches of Adolf Hitler*, edited by Norman H. Baynes, OUP, 1942)

On 2 August President Hindenburg died. Three hours later it was announced that Hitler had taken over his powers; the title of President was abolished and Hitler would be known as Führer and Chancellor. The cabinet had already agreed to it. The generals agreed that every army officer would swear an oath of loyalty to him.

Hitler's political domination was complete. He now began to extend it into every area of German life.

"Co-ordination": Events in Germany, 1933-39

Dictators need to control every feature of people's lives – they would control even their thoughts if they could. Anyone who thinks or acts independently of the party line is seen as a potential threat. In the six years between his rise to power as Chancellor and the start of the Second World War Hitler tried to organize or "co-ordinate" every aspect of German life to fit his Nazi views – and to keep the people so keyed up with new ideas and new experiences that they would have neither the time nor the desire to resist him.

EDUCATION

The Nazis take over German schools:

The German schools were quickly Nazified. Textbooks were hastily rewritten . . . all teachers took an oath to be loyal and obedient to Adolf Hitler. Later, no man could teach who had not first served in the SA, the Labour Service or the Hitler Youth . . . the teaching of the 'racial sciences' exalted the Germans as the master race and the Jews as the breeder of almost all the evil there was in the world.

(*Source: The Rise and Fall of the Third Reich*, William L. Shirer, Pan Books, 1964)

YOUTH MOVEMENTS

Membership of the Hitler Youth organization became compulsory in 1936. A series of separate organizations were set up for boys and girls, depending on their age. Each provided a mixture of sport, propaganda and competitive games.

The Führer addresses the Hitler Youth, 1934.

The Law on the Hitler Youth:

The future of the German nation depends upon its youth and German youth must therefore be prepared for its future duties. The Reich Government has accordingly decided on the following law which is published herewith:

1. The whole of German youth within the borders of the Reich is organised in the Hitler Youth.

2. All German young people, apart from being educated at home and at school, will be educated in the Hitler Youth physically, intellectually, and morally in the spirit of National Socialism to serve the nation and the community.

3. The task of educating German youth in the Hitler Youth is being entrusted to the Reich Leader of German Youth in the NSDAP. He therefore becomes the 'Youth Leader of the German Reich'.

(*Source:* Quoted in *Documents on Nazism 1919-45*, Noakes and Pridham)

Hitler addresses the Hitler Youth at Nuremburg, September 1935:

What we look for from our German youth is different from what people wanted in the past. In our eyes the German youth of the future must be slim and slender, swift as the greyhound, tough as leather, and hard as Krupp steel. We must educate a new type of man so that our people is not ruined by the symptoms of decadence.

(*Source:* Quoted in *Documents on Nazism 1919-45*, Noakes and Pridham)

CENSORSHIP   The Nazis set up "chambers" to censor and control all the mass media – newspapers, films, radio, etc. Authors who had produced books which went against Nazi ideas found them quickly disposed of.

A typical public book-burning:

All afternoon Nazi raiding parties had gone into public and private libraries, throwing on to the streets such books as Dr Goebbels in his supreme wisdom had decided were unfit for Nazi Germany. From the streets Nazi columns of beerhall fighters had picked up these discarded volumes and taken them to the square . . . here the heap grew higher and higher, and every few minutes another howling mob arrived. Then, as night fell . . . the flames began to soar skyward . . .

(*Source: The Goebbels Diaries 1942-3*, Louis P. Lochner, Washington DC, 1948)

NEWSPAPERS   **A Propaganda Ministry order to the press:**

6 iv 35: The Propaganda Ministry asks us to put to editors-in-chief the following requests, which must be observed in future with particular care:
   Photos showing members of the Reich Government at dining tables in front of rows of bottles must not be published in future . . . . Recently, the utterly absurd impression has been created among the public that members of the Government are living it up. News pictures must therefore change in this respect.

(*Source:* Quoted in *Documents on Nazism 1919-45*, Noakes and Pridham)

THE LAW   Hitler declared himself to be Germany's "supreme judge" and took powers to remove any judge whose sentences seemed too light, and to end the careers of lawyers who resisted Nazi attempts to interfere in political trials. He was anxious to keep the loyalty of the German workforce, despite abolishing the Trades Unions in 1933. The Labour Front (DAF) was officially supposed to protect the workers, but in practice it kept them under strict control. Wages were carefully regulated and a system of "workbooks" prevented an employee from changing firms if his previous employer wanted to keep him – although this did also give him security of employment.

"Strength through Joy"

[Hitler] came up with an organisation called *Kraft durch Freude* ("Strength through Joy"). This provided what can only be called regimented leisure

Hitler speaks at the laying of the foundation stone of the Volkswagen works, Wolfsburg, 1938.

... no organised social, sport or recreational group was allowed to function except under the control and direction of *Kraft durch Freude*. It provided ocean cruises and special skiing excursions ... bargain rate tickets to the theatre, the opera and the concerts ...

(*Source: The Rise and Fall of the Third Reich*, William L. Shirer, Pan Books, 1964)

The scheme also promised a very cheap "people's car" – the Volkswagen. Millions of workers made advance payments towards one, but few were ever delivered. No-one dared to protest. Many were grateful just to have a job at all – and many more now were in work, thanks to Hitler's massive schemes for rearmament, canal and motorway building and other huge projects.

Long before 1939, Hitler had the German people under almost total control. Resistance to his wishes had became almost impossible – as Part 6 shows. For those who had been out of work in 1933 but who now had jobs, life was very much better in many ways. But jobs had to be paid for, and finding enough money to pay the wages was a big problem for the Nazi government. Some historians even think that Hitler was forced to go to war in 1939 because the economy was running out of control – only seizing goods and factories abroad could solve his difficulty. Certainly, as the 1930s went on, his foreign policy became more and more adventurous.

THINGS TO DO AND THINK ABOUT:

See if you can find books in your library which show how Hitler used posters and photographs to win support. (The Imperial War Museum in London has an excellent selection for sale.)

What are the main ways in which governments nowadays can try to influence what we think and what we do?

Imagine that all your textbooks were full of political propaganda, and that your teachers were all determined to make you hold the same views as they did. How easy would it be for them to persuade you?

Foreign Policy and Rearmament

HITLER AND THE ARMY

From the earliest days of the Nazi Party, Hitler was determined to destroy the Versailles Treaty. Rapid rearmament would help him to achieve this, and he believed it would also win him favour with the generals; the army was the one organization with the potential power to overthrow him.

Hitler reassures the generals, 1933:

On February 2nd 1933, three days after assuming office, [Hitler] had made a two-hour address to the top generals and admirals at the house of General von Hammerstein, the Army commander-in-chief.... Admiral Raeder admitted that he was highly pleased at the prospect of a new navy, and General von Blomberg ... declared later that the Führer opened up 'a field of activities holding great possibilities for the future'.

(*Source: The Rise and Fall of the Third Reich*, William L. Shirer, Pan Books, 1964)

LEBENSRAUM

Hitler was also determined to win *Lebensraum* – "Living Space" – for the German people, which would satisfy their economic needs and reflect their superiority over other nations as the master-race. His immediate aim was to unite all German-speaking people into a single political unit.

From 1933-5 Hitler proceeded slowly in foreign affairs, anxious to seem reasonable and to avoid direct conflict with France. Early in 1934 he made a non-aggression pact with Poland, hoping to break the Poles' friendship with France and to win a political ally against Russia. Six months later there was a serious setback to his plans to unite Germany and Austria into a single state – Austrian Nazis shot and killed the Austrian Chancellor, Dollfuss. Mussolini reacted so strongly to the prospect of a united German/Austrian government on his doorstep that Hitler was forced to disown the coup attempt.

1935 began well for Germany. The people of the Saar region, which had been given to France for fifteen years at Versailles, voted decisively to return to Germany. Better still, the British entered into the Anglo-German naval agreement which not only offered Germany less strict armaments limitations than the Versailles Treaty but also drove a wedge between Britain and France. And when Mussolini invaded Abyssinia, Italy's earlier agreements with Britain and France collapsed as they protested about her action to the League of Nations. By early 1936, Hitler felt he could afford to be more daring: the Versailles Treaty had banned German troops from the land west of the River Rhine, but Hitler now marched in. The Allies, divided amongst themselves, and greatly overestimating Hitler's military strength, did nothing.

THE RHINELAND CRISIS

Hitler looks back on the Rhineland remilitarization:

Years later, reminiscing over the dinner table, Hitler asked 'What would have happened if anybody other than myself had been at the head of the Reich? Anyone you care to mention would have lost his nerve. I was obliged to lie . . . . I threatened unless the situation eased to send six extra divisions. The truth was, I had only four brigades. Next day, the English papers wrote that there had been an easing of the situation.'

(*Source: Hitler: A Study in Tyranny*, Alan Bullock, Pelican Books, 1962)

Later in the year, Hitler signed the Axis pact with Mussolini: the two dictators both sent help to General Franco who was fighting Communists in the Spanish Civil War. Much of 1937 was spent putting into operation the Four-Year Plan, designed to organize the German economy for a future war. Much inefficiency remained, and Göring was probably the wrong choice to mastermind it, but by late 1937 Hitler was keen to accelerate his aggressive policy.

HITLER UNVEILS HIS FUTURE PLANS

The Hossbach Conference, 1937:

Hitler's real plans came to light in the secret conference of 5 November 1937 . . . . It was the same old concept from which he had never strayed . . . only the tone of impatience was new . . . . All economic and social difficulties, all racial dangers, could be mastered only by overcoming the scarcity of space – the problem could no longer be solved by reaching out for overseas colonies . . . . It was his unalterable resolve to solve the question of German space between 1943 and 1945 at the latest . . . . He was determined to strike in 1938 without waiting . . . . This exposition evidently stunned and disturbed some of the group . . . .

(*Source: Hitler*, Joachim C. Fest, Pelican Books, 1977)

THE ANSCHLUSS

Four months later, Hitler invaded Austria, directly defying the Versailles Treaty which had forbidden the two countries to unite. Twenty-five years after slipping away from Austria poor and rejected, Hitler returned as a hero (see page 14). The secret police rounded up anyone who might resist, and in a referendum 99.75 per cent of Austria was said to have supported unity with Germany. Britain and France decided not to fight over it.

CZECHOSLOVAKIA

Hitler then turned to Czechoslovakia. He believed the Czechs to be inferior to Germans racially, and the boundaries drawn at Versailles meant that a long finger of their country jutted into the new Germany/Austria (see page 20). The Czechs had a fine army and the powerful Skoda steelworks – useful for rearmament. The area nearest Germany, the Sudetenland, had once been German territory and still contained many German-speaking people who were keen to join Hitler's empire. Hitler was quick to exploit this support and demanded that the Czech government hand over the Sudetenland.

Allied leaders, led by the new British Prime Minister, Neville Chamberlain, still believed that Hitler could be satisfied. Their policy was known as "appeasement" — giving concessions to keep the peace. Chamberlain flew to Germany to meet Hitler three times in September 1938. A conference of Hitler, Chamberlain, Mussolini and Daladier (for France) took place at Munich on 29 September.

A Punch *cartoon criticizes appeasement, 1938.*

LITTLE CZECH-RIDING-HOOD

" What sharp teeth you have, Grandmamma! "
" All the better for peacefully revising treaties, my dear."

THE MUNICH CONFERENCE

Czechoslovakia is left to its fate:

Czechoslovakians waited outside to learn their fate. An agreement was signed in the early hours of the next day. Hitler was allowed to occupy the Sudetenland, and a four-power commission would establish the new boundaries. Relations between Hitler and the foreigners were tolerably good. Chamberlain told him fishing stories. Daladier swapped anecdotes about the war. Hitler was full of contempt for them both and later called them "little worms". He himself drove into the Sudetenland and said the Munich agreement of September 30 was "an undreamt-of triumph, so great that you can scarcely imagine it". He had obtained the Czech defences without firing a shot.

(*Source: Hitler*, Norman Stone, Coronet Books, 1982)

Chamberlain received a hero's welcome when he returned to London. *The Times* remarked: "No conqueror returning from a victory on the battlefield has come home adorned with nobler laurels than Mr Chamberlain". But in March 1939 Hitler occupied Prague itself.

HITLER OCCUPIES PRAGUE

The Munich Treaty is torn up:

On Wednesday morning a communiqué was issued stating that the Führer had taken the Czech nation under the protection of the German Reich, with a guarantee of autonomous development of its natural life . . .

Snow was falling heavily when the Germans entered Prague but a crowd of several thousands were assembled in the Wenceslas Square. Many were weeping, and the people received the Germans with boos and jeers. Herr Hitler arrived in Prague at 7 o'clock . . .

(*Source: The Times Educational Supplement*, 18 March 1939)

The Allies had already decided that they could do nothing to stop him. But they were now rearming quickly, and they saw that his next move was likely to be against Poland and the Danzig Corridor (see page 20). Promises were made that Poland would be protected: talks were opened with the Russians to see if they might help. But on 22 August 1939, Hitler dropped a bombshell – he and the Russian leader Stalin agreed not to fight each other for the next twenty-five years. Armed with this guarantee, Hitler moved into Poland ten days later (see page 17). This time, the Allies decided to resist.

1939: BRITAIN DECLARES WAR

The scene in Berlin:

I was standing in the Wilhelmstrasse before the Chancellery about noon when the loudspeakers suddenly announced that Great Britain had declared herself at war with Germany. Some 250 people – no more – were standing there in the sun. They listened attentively to the announcement. When it was finished, there was not a murmur. They just stood there. Stunned. It was difficult for them to comprehend that Hitler had led them into a world war.

(*Source: The Rise and Fall of the Third Reich*, William L. Shirer, Pan Books, 1964)

THINGS TO DO AND THINK ABOUT:

Chamberlain described Czechoslovakia as "a far-off land of which we know nothing". Why do you think he was so unwilling to fight for her? (He was 70 years old in 1938 – what would he remember?)

Winston Churchill wrote angrily of the Munich Conference: "£1 was demanded at the pistol point. When it was given, £2 was demanded at the pistol point. Finally the dictator consented to take £1.17.6d . . .". What can you find out about Churchill's attitude to British government policy in the 1930s? What was he doing himself at this time?

German Resistance to Hitler

PROBLEMS OF EVIDENCE

It is extremely difficult to know how many Germans resisted the Nazi regime, either by merely disobeying or ignoring the government's orders when they could, or by actively trying to plot Hitler's downfall. It is also impossible to know how many members of the German Resistance died in the process. The Allies, who were contacted by Resistance members on a number of occasions, were naturally suspicious, fearing that such approaches were either a trap by Hitler's agents or merely a result of the fear that defeat in the war would bring Germany another harsh treaty. Nevertheless, there are many examples of great individual bravery. Bishop von Galen of Münster is one example. Goebbels said openly that he would like to have him hanged, but the bishop was too popular locally for the government to risk arresting him.

PROTESTS FROM THE CHURCH

A Church leader speaks out against euthenasia, 1941:

The first transport of innocent people who have been condemned to death has left Marienthal . . . . So we have to be prepared for these poor, helpless, sick people to be prematurely killed. Why? Not because they have committed a crime deserving death . . . . It is because in the opinion of some doctor or committee, they do not deserve to live, being "unproductive citizens" . . . woe to mankind, woe to our German people if God's holy commandment, Thou shalt not kill, is broken . . .

(*Source:* von Galen's sermon in the St Lambertini Church in Münster, 3 August 1941)

A protest against Jewish persecution:

After the violence of November 1938 [see page 15], the Dean of St Hedwig's [Berlin], Monsignor Bernhard Lichtenberg, called upon the congregations of the Berlin cathedral to pray "for Jews and inmates of concentration camps". This and other demonstrations, such as his protest against the "mercy killing" of mental patients led to his arrest in October, 1942. Whilst in prison he voluntarily applied for transfer to the ghetto at Lodz. He died on the way to Dachau in November, 1943.

(*Source: The German Opposition to Hitler*, H. Rothfels, Oswald Wolff, 1961)

There were many examples in the Protestant churches, too – notably amongst members of the Confessing Church led by Pastor Martin Niemöller.

STUDENTS PROTEST IN IN MUNICH

In 1943 the "White Rose" group of students at Munich University, led by Hans and Sophie Scholl, displayed leaflets all over the university buildings. They were tortured by the SS before execution.

The Declaration of the White Rose Group:

The time is coming for the youth of Germany to settle accounts with the most loathsome tyranny ever to be visited upon our people. In the name of German Youth we demand from this Adolf Hitler government the return of our personal freedom, our most treasured possession, which he has filched from us in the most despicable way.

(*Source:* Quoted in *Documents on Nazism 1919-45*, Noakes and Pridham)

PASSIVE RESISTANCE

Various political parties, abolished in 1933, tried to keep at least a gesture of protest going by organizing a whispering campaign against the government. There was little else they could do, given the efficiency of the police. Open resistance was impossible, so they organized themselves into small groups.

A Gestapo report on Socialist Party cells:

After work they join each other over a glass of beer, meet former kindred spirits near their homes, or keep in touch by means of family visits; they avoid all forms of organisation: and seek in the manner described to help their political friends remain steadfast. During these meetings, of course, there is talk about the political situation and news is exchanged. They promote energetically the whispering campaign . . . the main subjects of discussion are price increases, low wages, economic exploitation of the people, freedom, shortage of raw materials, corruption . . . and so on. Since many former SPD and trade union officials are now commercial travellers and travelling salesmen, such catchwords will spread comparatively quickly into the furthest parts of the Reich. Despite the extent of these subversive activities it has not yet been possible to catch a single one of these persons in the act and bring him to trial.

(*Source:* Quoted in *Documents on Nazism 1919-45*, Noakes and Pridham)

THE JULY BOMB PLOT

But the only really concerted show of resistance was the July Plot of 1944. The army had always been the one organization in Germany with the power to overthrow Hitler, but its most senior officers had either remained loyal to Hitler or were too hesitant to plan his removal. However, a group of army officers did take the initiative in 1944. A bomb was planted in a briefcase under Hitler's conference table. It injured him much more severely than official Nazi reports admitted, but it did not kill him and over the following months he exacted a terrible revenge. Gestapo records list 7,000 arrests; nearly 5,000 Germans were executed.

The official announcement about the Plot:

An attempt on the life of Hitler was made yesterday . . . the following announcement was made by the German News Agency last night:
'An attempt on the life of the Führer was made with high explosives today . . . . Hitler received slight burns and concussion, but no injuries. He at once began to work again. He then received Mussolini for a long meeting as previously arranged . . .' After reading the official

announcement which was broadcast on all German wireless stations, the newsreader said: 'There is nobody in Germany who does not feel a sense of deep gratitude that the Führer has escaped uninjured . . .'

(*Source: The Times*, 21 July 1944)

THINGS TO DO AND THINK ABOUT:

Imagine that you are a member of a group planning an attempt on Hitler's life. What will be the main problems that you will have in carrying out the plan?

Find out the full story of the July Plot. Why do you think the Nazis were so anxious to play down the results of the bomb blast?

What reasons can you think of for the decision to carry out the July Plot? Do you think hatred of Hitler was the only motive?

Hitler and the Jews

There was a large number of anti-Jewish groups in Germany, Austria and other countries at the beginning of this century, but Hitler's views, and his "solution" to what he called the Jewish "problem", were more extreme than any. Look back at his comments on the Jews in Vienna on page 28. He also thought that they had undermined the German war effort in 1914-18, and blamed them for the hated treaty and republic which followed the war. He saw the British and American governments as both manipulated by Jews. Above all, he believed that Jews were biologically inferior to the blond, Aryan, German race, fit only for slavery in large tracts of Eastern Europe, or for death.

Hitler's early views on extermination:

If, at the beginning of the [First World] war and during the war, twelve or fifteen thousand of these Hebrew defilers had been put under poison gas, as thousands of our very best workers from all walks of life had to endure at the front, then the sacrifice of millions at the front would not have been in vain. On the contrary: twelve thousand scoundrels eliminated in time might perhaps have saved the lives of a million decent valuable Germans.

(*Source: Mein Kampf*, Adolf Hitler, Hutchinson, 1969)

To whom is Hitler referring when he speaks of "millions at the front"? Why does he mention poison gas?

Once Hitler came to power, persecution of the Jews can be divided into four stages.

1933-35 Discrimination against Jews was petty and often unofficial, for example to ban them from certain shops. Sometimes the new Nazi government actually told local SA groups not to be so violent towards Jews. The first concentration camps appeared at Dachau and elsewhere – but there was no mass extermination yet.

An American reports on anti-Jewish outrages, 1933:

In Dresden several weeks ago uniformed 'Nazis' raided the Jewish Prayer House, interrupted the evening religious service, arrested twenty-five worshippers, and tore the holy insignia or emblems from their head-covering worn while praying.

Eighteen Jewish shops, including a bakery, mostly in Chemnitz, had their windows broken by rioters led by uniformed 'Nazis'.

Five of the Polish Jews arrested in Dresden were each compelled to drink one-half-litre of castor oil . . .

(*Source:* Reports by Ralph Busser, American Consul in Leipzig, 5 April 1933, quoted in *Documents on Nazism 1919-45*, Noakes and Pridham)

The Nazi newspaper orders a boycott of Jewish shops:

The principle is: No German must any longer buy from a Jew or let him and his backers promote their goods . . . . Orders are being sent to the SA and the SS so that from the moment of the boycott the population will be warned by guards not to enter Jewish shops.

(*Source: Völkischer Beobachter*, 29 March 1933)

1935-37 The SS gradually took over the task of action against the Jews. Laws began to be passed which excluded Jews from whole areas of German life and types of work. Jews were legally classified as inferior citizens. There was a brief lull in 1936; Hitler wanted to keep the persecution secret at a time when many foreigners were visiting Berlin for the Olympic Games (see page 10).

The Reich Citizenship Law, 1935:

A Jew cannot be a citizen of the Reich. He has no right to vote in political affairs, and he cannot hold public office . . . . A Jew is anyone who is descended from at least three grandparents who are racially full Jews.

(*Source:* Quoted in *Documents on Nazism, 1919-45*, Noakes and Pridham)

1938-40 Hitler believed the whole "problem" was getting more urgent as the war began. After Germany invaded Poland, Hitler used Poland as a dumping-ground for large numbers of Jews who were forcibly removed from Germany.

1941-45 The systematic killing of Jews began at Auschwitz and elsewhere. These new camps were specially built so that able-bodied Jews could be forced to work until they were so weak that the SS could kill them in gas chambers designed to eliminate as many people in as short a time as possible.

The testimony of the Auschwitz commandant at the Nuremburg trials, 1946:

I was ordered to establish the extermination facilities at Auschwitz in June 1941. The camp commandant [at Treblinka] used monoxide gas, and I did not think that his methods were very efficient. So at Auschwitz I used Cyclon B . . . . It took from three to fifteen minutes to kill the people in the chamber, according to climatic conditions. We knew when the people were dead because their screaming stopped. We usually waited about half an hour before we opened the doors and removed the bodies. After the bodies were removed, our special commandos took off the rings and extracted the gold from the teeth of the corpses. Another improvement that we made over Treblinka was that we built our gas chambers to accommodate two thousand people at one time . . .

(*Source:* Nuremburg Documents 1918, quoted in *Hitler and the Nazis*, D.M. Phillips, The Archive Series, Hill and Fell, 1968)

BBC correspondent Richard Dimbleby enters Belsen, 1945:

I passed through the barrier and found myself in the whirl of a nightmare. Dead bodies, some of them in decay, lay strewn about the road and along the rutted tracks. On each side of the road were brown wooden huts. There were faces at the windows, the emaciated faces of starving women too weak to come outside, propping themselves against the glass to see the daylight before they died. And they were dying every hour and every minute. I saw a man wandering dazedly along the road, stagger and fall. Someone else looked down at him, took him by the heels and dragged him to the side of the road to join the other bodies lying unburied there. No-one else took the slightest notice; they didn't even trouble to turn their heads. Inside the huts it was even worse. I have seen many terrible sights in the last five years, but nothing, nothing approaching the dreadful interior of this hut at Belsen.

The dead and the dying lay close together. I picked my way over corpse after corpse in the gloom until I heard one voice that rose above the gentle undulating moaning. I found a girl – she was a living skeleton; it was impossible to gauge her age for she had practically no hair left on her head and her face was only a yellow parchment sheet with two holes in it for eyes. She was stretching out her sticks of arms and gasping something. It was "Englisch! Englisch! Medizin! Medizin!" And she was trying to cry but had not enough strength.

(*Source:* BBC Record, *History 1917-71*)

Some people have suggested that Hitler himself had Jewish blood and that his hatred of the Jews was part of an obsession to keep that fact secret. We cannot be sure, just as we cannot be certain that he had always planned this terrible "final solution". He probably had a general idea rather than a precise plan, and drew up his timetable as events unfolded in the 1930s. What we can be sure about is that the suffering was terrible.

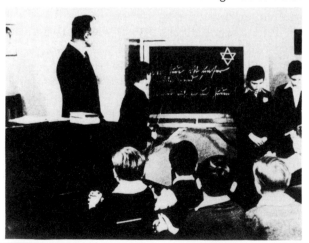

The Jewish boys are humiliated in front of members of their class. The words on the blackboard say: "The Jew is our greatest enemy! Beware of the Jews!"

Epilogue – 1939-45

Hitler invaded Poland on 1 September 1939, and Britain declared war on Germany two days later. Despite some breakdowns in communications and equipment, everything went very well for Hitler at first; Germany and Russia shared out Poland in the autumn and, in April 1940, the German army occupied Denmark and most of Norway. A month later, the Germans marched through Holland and Belgium and on to France; Paris fell on 13 June. The British were forced to evacuate over 300,000 troops from mainland Europe at Dunkirk. For several weeks in the summer the British, now led by Winston Churchill, stood alone as the Battle of Britain took place over the Channel. Later in the year Hitler began his blitz bombing of British cities. In 1941 he felt confident enough to attack Russia, despite his earlier alliance with Stalin.

But in 1942 the tide began to turn. Long before the invasion of Poland, Hitler had been warned by his military experts against getting involved in a long-drawn-out struggle. But the Americans had entered the war when the Japanese attacked Pearl Harbor. Hitler had to send help to Mussolini in

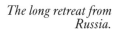
The long retreat from Russia.

North Africa, but was unable to prevent the defeat at El Alamein in November. In January 1943 93,000 Germans were forced to surrender to the Russians at Stalingrad; the Russian winter killed thousands more. Within eighteen months the Allies had invaded North Africa and Italy, then France on D-Day. On every front the Germans were forced back. 100,000 Germans died as the Allies bombed Dresden in 1945.

By the start of 1945, the position was clearly hopeless. German armies were in rapid retreat abroad. At home, the Nazi government, never very efficiently organized, was rapidly disintegrating into bitter arguments between its various departments.

The war meant that Hitler had to cut his public appearances dramatically. He showed that he had lost none of his old skill at persuading his audience that they should support him, but by early 1942 the strain of the war, especially in Russia, was clearly affecting his health. Goebbels noticed how much he had aged, that he complained of giddiness and said that even the sight of snow made him physically sick. A year later he was suffering trembling fits in his left arm and leg; a small growth had to be removed from his vocal cords and he was relying more and more on drugs prescribed for him by Dr Morell, his sinister doctor whose medical skills were highly questionable.

His life became more and more lonely; he went out into the fresh air less and less. "He sits in his bunker, worries and broods," said Goebbels. The July Bomb Plot of 1944 injured him significantly; according to William Shirer, "his hair had been singed, his legs burned, his right arm bruised and temporarily paralysed, his eardrums punctured and his back lacerated by a falling beam". The shock must have been considerable.

After a breakdown in September 1944 his rages became terrible. General Guderian was on the receiving end of a rage that lasted over two hours. "His fists raised, his cheeks flushed with rage . . . having lost all self-control. He was almost screaming, his eyes seemed to pop out of his head and the veins stood out in his temples." He increasingly deluded himself about the true state of the war, relying on some last-minute miracle to save him and looking for it "in the stars". Fearful of being poisoned by someone in his immediate circle, he ordered all food to be tasted before he himself ate it.

By March 1945 those around him noted that Hitler had become an old man, totally exhausted. He returned from the Eastern Front headquarters at Rastenburg to his bunker in the middle of Berlin, fifty feet below ground. On 19 March he ordered that all factories, bridges, lorries, railway rolling stock and supply depots should be destroyed so that they did not fall into enemy hands. The order was largely ignored. After briefly convincing himself that the sudden death of American President Roosevelt on 12 April was the turning point that he had been waiting for, he realized that the end had come.

On 29 April he drew up his last Will and Testament, defending his past actions and declaring his intention to commit suicide. Göring and Himmler were expelled from the movement for trying to open secret talks with the Allies and, remembering the treachery of the army in July 1944, Hitler appointed the Navy Chief, Admiral Dönitz, as his successor. The next day he shot himself in the bunker and his mistress, Eva Braun, took poison. A week later, Germany surrendered. Many leading Nazis fled abroad, especially to South America. Others, like Himmler, committed suicide. Those leading Nazis still alive were put on trial at Nuremburg in 1946; ten were hanged, but Göring managed to take poison only hours before his execution was due. 1500 others received the death sentence in other trials.

Germany was occupied by the Allies. Britain, France, America and Russia divided the country into zones; in due course the Russian zone became the modern East Germany, fenced off from the West by the Iron Curtain and the Berlin Wall.

Hitler's regime was one of the most evil that the world has ever known. There were many evil dictators before him, and no doubt there will be many more. But in one respect, Hitler is quite unlike earlier ones. Albert Speer, Hitler's armaments minister, was released after a twenty-year gaol sentence and wrote a book in which he recalled what he had said at the Nuremburg trials:

Hitler's dictatorship employed to perfection the instruments of technology to dominate its own people . . . by such instruments as the radio and public-address systems, eighty million persons could be made subject to the will of one individual . . . to transmit the commands of the highest levels direct to the lowest where they were carried out uncritically . . . to maintain a close watch over all citizens and to keep criminal operations shrouded in a high degree of secrecy . . . . Dictatorship of the past needed assistants of high quality in the lower ranks of leadership also – men who could think and act independently. The authoritarian system in the age of technology can do without such men.

So Hitler's government and party depended entirely on the Führer himself. Its failure and inefficiencies were a direct result of his dictatorial style of leadership. It is not surprising therefore that the regime and its leaders went down together.

THINGS TO DO AND THINK ABOUT:

Do you think control of the media is a sufficient explanation for Hitler's success?

Sources

Great problems are involved in dealing with original documents on the Nazi period. Apart from the obvious language problems for those who do not speak fluent German, many of the documents were either banned or falsified by the Nazis themselves, or destroyed in Allied bombing raids during the war. For a long period after 1945 books like *Mein Kampf* were scarcely reprinted at all, partly because people wanted to lay the past to rest and partly for fear of encouraging Nazi-style groups to spring up elsewhere. It is still very difficult to obtain English reprints of Nazi newspapers. For all these reasons, this book relies heavily on collections of documents or secondary accounts of events.

Nazi documents are not easy to interpret, even if you do understand the language. They tend to be long-winded and full of obscure, long words, and to contain arguments that are arranged in no logical order and which merely ramble round in circles. Hitler's book *Mein Kampf* is a prime example of this.

There is also the question of bias. Is it humanly possible for anyone to examine coolly and objectively cruelty on the scale on which Hitler practised it? Is it possible for a historian who is Jewish to write in an unbiased way about the Nazi regime? Can any German who lived through Hitler's reign of terror avoid the charge that he is merely seeking to excuse or explain away past actions? And can any Allied historian who lived through the war and wrote about its events soon afterwards be completely free from such distortion?

GENERAL COLLECTIONS OF DOCUMENTS
The best single collection, extensively used in preparing this book, is *Documents on Nazism, 1919-1945* by Jeremy Noakes and Geoffrey Pridham. These appear in a single-volume hardback (Jonathan Cape, 1974) and are gradually appearing in three paperback volumes (Exeter Studies in History). *Hitler and the Rise of the Nazis* by D.M. Phillips (The Archive Series, Hill and Fell, 1968) is a good, brief selection; others can be found in two books in the Longman "Seminar Studies in History" series – *The Weimar Republic* by J.W. Hiden (1974) and *The Third Reich* by D.G. Williamson (1982) together with explanatory narrative. Two notable recent additions are *Weimar Germany* and *Hitler's Germany* both by Josh Brooman (Longman); *Germany* by Robert Gibson and Jon Nichol (Blackwell) will also be very useful.

FIRST-HAND ACCOUNTS
The Rise and Fall of the Third Reich by William L. Shirer (Pan Books, 1964) is the leading account from an Allied journalist; Chapter 8 on the home policies of the Nazis will be especially useful. See also Shirer's *Berlin Diary* (two volumes, Bantam Books, 1986). *Inside the Third Reich* by Albert Speer (Macmillan, 1970) is a highly interesting account by one of Hitler's leading ministers, but naturally needs to be treated with caution. *Mein Kampf* by Adolf Hitler (Hutchinson, 1969) is available in a number of different editions.

GENERAL HISTORIES
Hitler. A Study in Tyranny by Alan Bullock (Pelican, 1962) is still the leading narrative, especially on Hitler's foreign policy. Of the more recent literature, *Hitler* by Norman Stone (Coronet, 1982) is a very racy and readable account, although for more detail there are *Hitler* by Joachim C. Fest (Pelican, 1977) and *Adolf Hitler* by John Toland (Doubleday, 1976). B.J. Elliott's *Hitler and Germany* and *Western Europe after Hitler* (Longman Modern Times, 1966/1968) are excellent briefer narratives, and Gordon Craig's *Germany 1866-1945* (OUP, 1978) is both clear and very informative.

PHOTOGRAPHS
Many selections are available in book form, notably *The Illustrated History of the Third Reich* by John Bradley, *Adolf Hitler* edited by Herbert Walther, and *Hitler's Propaganda Machine* by Ward Rutherford (all Bison Books, 1978) and *The Hitler Years* by Ivor Mantanle (Galley Press, 1984).

BIOGRAPHIES OF INDIVIDUAL NAZIS
Encyclopaedia of the Third Reich by Louis L. Snyder (Robert Hale, 1976) and *Who's Who in Nazi Germany* by Robert Wistrich (Weidenfeld and Nicolson, 1982) give brief entries on all the leading figures. These are expanded in a series of interesting essays in *The Face of the Third Reich* by Joachim C. Fest (Penguin Books, 1979).

THE WEIMAR REPUBLIC
The literature is not easy. *The Kings Depart* by Richard M. Watt (Weidenfeld and Nicolson, 1969) describes the Republic's turbulent birth. The volumes by Hiden and Brooman (see above), *Germany 1918-1933* by Simon Taylor (Duckworth, 1983) and *Weimar and the Rise of Hitler* by A.J. Nicholls (Papermac, 1968) are also useful.

THE STYLE AND POLICIES OF THE NAZI GOVERNMENT
These too are far from simple to read. *The German Dictatorship* by K.D. Bracher (Peregrine, 1978) and *The Hitler State* by Martin Broszat (Longman, 1981) are detailed surveys, along with *Hitler: The Führer and the People* by J.P. Stern (Fontana/Collins, 1975). Economic policies are expounded in *The Nazi Economic Policy* by R.J. Overy (Macmillan, 1982), while *Government, Party and People in Nazi Germany* edited by Jeremy Noakes (Exeter Studies in History) examines the areas from which Hitler drew his support. A useful survey of foreign policy controversies can be found in *The Origins of*

the *Second World War* edited by Esmonde M. Robertson (Macmillan, 1971). For Hitler's Jewish policies Lucy Dawidowicz's *The War against the Jews* (Pelican, 1977) is a truly awesome, detailed narrative.

RESISTANCE
For general accounts, see *The German Resistance to Hitler* by Hermann Graml and others (Batsford, 1970) and *The German Opposition to Hitler* by Hans Rothfels (Oswald Wolff, 1961). Both Bullock and Shirer contain accounts of the 1944 Plot – see also *The July Plot* by Roger Manzell and Heinrich Fraenkel (The Bodley Head, 1964) and the *The July Plot* by Nigel Richardson (Dryad Press, 1986). Army resistance generally is described in *The Nemesis of Power* by Sir John Wheeler Bennett (Macmillan, 1953) and *The German Army 1933-45* by Albert Seaton (Weidenfeld and Nicolson, 1982).

Biographies

CHAMBERLAIN, Neville (1869-1940)
British Prime Minister 1937-40. Chamberlain was born into a great political family; his father Joseph and half-brother Austen were both Conservative cabinet ministers. Chamberlain served for a long time in Birmingham local government, becoming Lord Mayor in 1916, then an MP, Postmaster General and Minister of Health before a notably successful period in the 1930s as Chancellor of the Exchequer. As Prime Minister he was determined to avoid a repeat of the horrible suffering of 1914-18, and believed Hitler could be "appeased" or satisfied – hence his appeasement policy of making concessions to Germany (which also bought time for Britain to rearm). By 1940 his party had lost confidence in him; when Hitler invaded Scandinavia he was forced to make way for Winston Churchill to become Prime Minister. He died shortly afterwards.

GOEBBELS, Paul Joseph (1897-1945)
Brought up in a strict Catholic family, Goebbels was the most intellectually skilful of the leading Nazis. He became obsessed with the fact that he was unable to serve in the First World War, owing to a crippled foot. He joined the Nazis in the early 1920s, writing for its newspapers and making brilliant speeches against Jews, Communists and the Weimar Republic. Hitler appointed him Reich Propaganda Leader in 1929 and he showed a brilliant mastery of persuasion techniques in the elections before Hitler came to power, and in controlling newspapers, films, theatre, cinema and radio thereafter. He was one of Hitler's closest advisers, working tirelessly to keep the war effort going in the dark days of 1943-5, and playing a leading role in the defeat of the July Plotters in 1944. Appointed Hitler's successor as Reich Chancellor in 1945, he poisoned his wife and six children and then killed himself in Hitler's bunker.

HIMMLER, Heinrich (1900-1945)
Head of the SS, and one of the most ruthless of the Nazis, yet a man who was physically sick when he himself had to witness the violence for which he was responsible. He became extremely powerful as a result of the massacre of the SA in 1934 and played a major role in the increasing persecution of the Jews after 1938, and in their mass extermination from 1941, organizing the death camps and supervising the occupation of Russia. By the end of the war he was the second most powerful man in Germany after Hitler, but was disowned by the Führer for trying to make contact with the Allies when he saw that all was lost. After Hitler's death, Himmler tried to flee from Germany but was captured by British troops. He managed to kill himself by swallowing a cyanide capsule while being examined by a doctor.

VON HINDENBURG, General Paul (1847-1934)
Germany's outstanding general in the 1914-18 war, and President of the Weimar Republic 1925-34. His victories against Russia made him a national hero in the First World War, but he was unable to stop the gradual collapse of German forces on the Western Front after being transferred there in 1916. Hindenburg was not in favour of Hitler becoming Chancellor and described him as "that little Bohemian corporal", but his own increasing old age and the deepening economic and political crises of 1929-33 made it impossible for him to prevent it in the end. Although treated with respect by Hitler, he played little part in events in 1933-4, and Hitler was well-prepared to seize total power when Hindenburg died in August 1934.

HITLER, Adolf (1889-1945)
Leader of the Third Reich 1933-45. After spending his early life in Austria in considerable poverty, he joined the German army in 1914 and rose to the rank of corporal,

winning the Iron Cross, First Class, for reasons unknown. After the war he founded the Nazi Party to restore German greatness, to overturn the Versailles Treaty and to "rid the world" of the Jews. An attempt to seize power in 1923 in Munich was a complete failure, but the world depression after 1929 and Hitler's own brilliance at propaganda techniques brought him to power in January 1933. Thereafter he conducted a reign of terror at home, while almost ending unemployment through huge government spending, and an increasingly aggressive foreign policy, leading to the Second World War in 1939. After considerable success in 1939-41, his invasion of Russia and the entry of the USA into the war made Germany's eventual defeat inevitable. With Germany in ruins in April 1945, Hitler committed suicide in his bunker in Berlin.

RÖHM, Ernst (1887-1934)

Like Himmler and many of the Nazi leadership, Röhm came from Bavaria. A professional soldier who revelled in wartime life in 1914-18, he joined the Freikorps when peace came and joined the plot which overthrew the left-wing government in this home state. He was at Hitler's side in the Munich putsch of 1923, but was quickly released after the trial, and went to Bolivia for five years as a military instructor. Called back by Hitler in 1930, he recruited more than two million men into the SA within three years, but was bitterly hated by gentlemen army officers. He criticized Hitler for his failure to introduce more socialist policies. When Hitler wiped out the SA in 1934, Röhm refused the chance to kill himself and was shot down by the SS. The homosexual Röhm described himself as "an immature and wicked man"; he was also the only one of Hitler's followers to address him by the familiar German form *Du*.

SPEER, Albert (1905-1981)

An architect by training, Speer joined the Nazi Party in 1931 and the SS a year later. He became Hitler's personal architect and city planner, as well as stage-managing a number of party rallies in the 1930s. From 1937 he set about redesigning Berlin, and was made Minister of Armaments and War Production in 1941, a post in which he achieved miracles in the production of armaments. He was tried at Nuremburg in 1946, and served a twenty-year prison sentence. *Inside the Third Reich*, his major book, was published in 1970; he died in London eleven years later while on a visit to give a television interview.

Glossary

Allies	those countries opposed to Germany – generally taken to mean Britain, France, the United States and Russia
anarchy	absence of government; disorder or confusion. An anarchist believes all governments should be destroyed
annex	*either* an additional clause to a treaty *or* to join one country to another by force
Anschluss	the take-over of Austria by Germany, March 1938
Aryan	the racial group comprising Germans and certain other North European peoples, believed by Hitler to be completely superior to the Jews
authoritarian	strongly disciplined; demanding obedience
autonomous	self-governing; independent
Bolshevism	Communism; movement supporting Lenin's revolution in Russia
bourgeois	predictably middle class; a term of disapproval, used by Nazis to pour scorn on their opponents
capitulation	surrender
Centre Party	political party supported by many German Roman Catholics and which represented the interests of that Church in parliament
Chancellor	approximate equivalent of British Prime Minister; head of the cabinet
coalitions	formal alliances between political parties
Communist	believes in all property being owned by the community rather than by individuals
constitution	method or arrangements by which a state is governed
contracting parties	individuals or groups signing an agreement
coup (d'état)	illegal seizure of power
creed	set of beliefs
democracy/democratic	government by the people, either directly or through chosen representatives
Depression	period of economic hardship in America and Europe after 1929
dictatorship	government by one man or one party, tolerating no disagreement and suppressing democracy
dissidents	those who disagree with the policies of the government
euthenasia	the act of killing someone, usually painlessly, in order to relieve pain during an incurable illness. The Nazis practised it on those whom they regarded as racially inferior, especially Jews.
Führer	leader; the official title which Hitler gave himself in 1934
Gauleiter	highest-ranking Nazi official below the top leadership. Appointed directly by Hitler, and responsible for all major activities in a given region (*Gau*)
Gestapo	secret police force designed to keep the Nazis in power
ghetto	area of a city reserved for a certain category or race of people, usually Jews
Heil Hitler	the traditional Nazi method of greeting someone
inquisitional tribune	examining court, supposedly supported by the people
Kellogg Pact	international agreement of 1928 signed by fifteen nations, rejecting war as a means of achieving their aims. Germany was one of those who signed.
League of Nations	international organization set up in Geneva after the First World War to prevent war and to encourage international cooperation. It had no army or police of its own, and was able to do little in practice against an aggressive leader like Hitler or Mussolini.
liberal	democratic, unprivileged, on behalf of the people
Marxist	follower of Karl Marx; believer in Communism, enforced by government with no "free" elections
mobilization	preparing for war
Nuremburg Trials	trials of leading Nazis held by an international court set up in Nuremburg after the war. Ten Nazis were hanged in October 1946; seven received prison sentences; three were acquitted. Many other trials of less important figures were held elsewhere.

Obergruppenführer	senior rank in the SA
pacifist	someone who believes that going to war is always wrong, whatever the reason for it.
pact	agreement
parliamentary bloc	group of individuals or parties voting together
patriotism	strong belief in supporting your country, whatever the circumstances
President	head of state; officially neutral politically, seeing that the Constitution is upheld
propaganda	biased information designed to win people over to a certain point of view
proportional representation	a system of elections in which all the votes are added together in order to calculate shares of seats for each party. There are several different variations. Significantly different from the British system of voting by constituencies.
Prussia	the leading state within Germany
Putsch	illegal seizure of power
radical	extreme
referendum	a national vote for or against a specific porposal
Reich	empire
Reichstag	Parliament
reparations	sums of money to be paid in compensation for damage and suffering in the First World War
Republican	type of government carried on by elected representatives of the people with no monarchy. The word can also be used to describe supporters of such a system
socialist	believer in state ownership of many industries and some compulsory redistribution of wealth from the rich to the poor. Differs from Communists in supporting free elections.
sovereignty	exercise of power
Spartakists	the forerunners of the German Communist Party
Stuka	a type of German war plane
swastika	Nazi symbol: crooked cross
synagogue	Jewish place of worship

Date List

1918	End of First World War.
1919	Treaty of Versailles.
	Weimar Republic set up.
	Hitler joins the German Workers' Party.
1922	French invade the Ruhr.
1923	Hitler's Munich Putsch fails.
1924	Hitler released from prison.
1928	Nazis win 12 seats in Reichstag elections.
1929	Wall Street Crash. Economic depression in Germany follows.
1930	Nazis win 107 seats.
1932	Nazis win 230 seats in July election.
1933	Hitler comes to power as Chancellor.
1934	Röhm's stormtroopers massacred in the Night of the Long Knives.
	President Hindenburg dies; Hitler becomes Führer and President.
	Nazi Putsch in Austria fails.
1935	Nuremburg laws against the Jews.
1936	Hitler remilitarizes the Rhineland.
	Olympic Games held in Berlin.
1938	Hitler invades Austria; occupies Sudetenland after the Munich Peace Conference.
	Crystalnight violence against the Jews.
1939	Hitler occupies Western Czechoslovakia.
	Hitler invades Poland; Britain and France declare war.
1940	Hitler invades Scandinavia; Churchill becomes British Prime Minister.
	Allied troops evacuated from France at Dunkirk.
1941	Hitler invades Russia.
	USA enters the war.
1942	Mass extermination of the Jews is stepped up.
1943	Allied troops invade Italy from North Africa.
1944	July Bomb Plot against Hitler fails.
1945	Hitler commits suicide in Berlin. Germany surrenders.
	End of Third Reich.

Index

Abyssinia 45
Allied reaction
  over Austria 16-17, 46
  over Czechoslovakia 16-17, 46-8
  over Poland 17, 48
  to Hitler generally 5, 9, 45, 49, 56
  to pre-Nazi Germany 22
Alsace-Lorraine 19
Army, German 9, 13, 41, 45-6, 55
Austria 14, 16, 45, 46, 52

Bavaria 30-1, 40-1
Berlin 3, 10, 30
Bismarck, Otto von 18
Blomberg, Werner von 13-14, 45
Braun, Eva 56
Brüning, Heinrich 33, 37

Centre Party 3, 33, 40
Chamberlain, Neville 5, 17, 46-8, 59
Christianity/churches 6, 49
Churchill, Winston 48, 55
Communist Party 6, 11, 16, 18, 31, 33,
  37, 39-40
concentration camps 7, 49, 53-4
"coordination" 42-4
Crystalnight 15
Czechoslovakia 15-16, 46-8, 52

Dachau 7, 49, 52
Danzig Corridor 17, 19, 48
Dönitz, Karl 56
Düsseldorf Industry Club 33

Ebert, Friedrich 23-4
economic affairs
  pre-Hitler 25-7, 33
  under Hitler 11, 44, 46
election results 24-5, 33, 37, 39-40, 41
Enabling Act 6, 7, 40

"Final Solution" 54
First World War 18, 52
France 27, 45, 55
Freikorps 24, 30
Fritsch, Werner Freiherr von 13-14
Führer, title of 9, 41

Gauleiters/Gaus 31
Goebbels, Paul Joseph 11, 37, 43, 49,
  56, 59
Göring, Hermann 11, 13-14, 30, 46, 56

Hamburg 3, 34
Himmler, Heinrich 4, 56, 59
Hindenburg, Paul von 9, 37, 38-9, 41, 59
Hitler, Adolf
  early life/career 28-32
  health/death 56
Hitler Youth 42-3
Hugenberg, Alfred 33

Jews
  Hitler's views on 28-9, 52
  treatment of 5, 9-11, 15, 49, 52-4
July Plot 50-1, 56

Kapp, Wolfgang 24
Kellogg Pact 27

Labour Front (DAF) 43
League of Nations 27, 45
Lebensraum 18, 45-6, 52
"Legal Revolution" 31, 37
Listener, The (magazine) 4
local government 40
Locarno Treaty 17

Mark, value of 25-6, 31
mass media 4, 12, 43, 57
Mein Kampf 28, 31-2
Munich
  Conference 1938 46-8
  Putsch 1923 27
Mussolini, Benito 45, 46-8, 50, 55

Night of the Long Knives 8, 41
Nuremburg
  Laws 9, 53
  Trials 56

one-party state 7, 40, 50, 57
Olympic Games 1936 10-11, 53

Papen, Franz von 37-8
People's Court 12
Poland 5, 16-17, 19, 45, 53, 55
Potempa murders 35
propaganda 12, 30, 34, 43, 57
proportional representation 24-5, 27
Punch magazine 37, 47

rallies 13, 30, 33-4, 38
rearmament 4, 11, 41, 45
Reichstag
  general 6, 25, 33, 37-8

fire 1933 39
reparations 20, 33
resistance to Hitler 5, 49-51
Rhineland 10, 20, 45-6
Ribbentrop, Joachim von 16
Röhm, Ernst 8, 30, 41, 60
Roosevelt, Franklin D. 56
Ruhr, French invasion of 27, 31
Russia 16, 23, 48, 55

SA 6, 7, 8, 33, 35, 39, 40, 41, 52-3
SS/Gestapo 6, 7, 8, 31, 33, 40, 44, 46,
  50, 53
Saar 19
Schleicher, Kurt von 38
schools 35, 42
Second World War 3, 55-7
Social Darwinism 28
Spanish Civil War 46
Spartakist revolt 27
Speer, Albert 11, 56-7, 60
Stalin, Joseph 16, 48, 55
Strasser
  Gregor 38
  Otto 31
"Strength through Joy" 43
Stresemann, Gustav 27
Sudetenland 15, 46-7

Times, The 22, 24, 47-8
trades unions 43

unemployment 16, 26-7, 33

Versailles Treaty
  terms 17, 18-22
  opposition to 25, 41
  Hitler's view of 5, 6, 9, 16, 30, 33,
    45-6
Vienna 28, 52
Volkswagen 44

Wall Street Crash 33
Weimar Republic
  constitution 24, 37-9
  Hitler's view of 6, 31, 38-9
  problems faced by 23, 25-7, 37-8
Wels, Otto 7
White Rose group 49-50
Wilhelm II 18

Young Plan 33